CW01642411

# THE GUT

Gateway to Health

Marion Schaatsbergen

# The Gut

## GATEWAY TO HEALTH

**Eliminate the harmful biofilm from your gut and reclaim your *vitality*, *radiance*, and *energy***

b:k light

ISBN 9789492595638

More information: www.marionschaatsbergen.com

Editing: BoekenBusiness.com
Design: Studio Mol
Translation: Textwerk

Translated from Dutch, original title: *De Darm, poort naar gezondheid* by Marion Schaatsbergen, ISBN 9789492595515, published by Booklight.nl



www.booklight.eu

b:k light

# Testimonials

With this new book by Marion Schaatsbergen, you have an excellent source, inspiration and the whole range of experiences at your disposal. With her profound knowledge, her intelligent approach and her experience from a dedicated life as a healer, Marion stands for everything that seems important and right to me in my life.

Not only did Marion bring this special and unique form of cleaning the small intestine and removing the biofilm to so many people who were looking for help to better health, but she is also committed to educating people about the background and connections that can affect their health – both negatively and positively. Without wanting to belittle the merits of medicine, I believe that the future of maintaining health, but also of healing from illnesses, increasingly lies in people's personal responsibility.

The intestinal detox cure is a milestone for all people who strive for better health. Let this book inspire you to take your health back into your own hands! The explanations in words and pictures are not only impart knowledge and enlighten, but they serve the deep understanding of the miracle of man.

Marion is much more than just an accompaniment on the way to health and vitality. This book describes these processes in a simple and understandable way. You will inevitably be inspired to try this form of colon cleansing. And I can only congratulate you on that!

You are taking the first step towards better well being as Marion describes it: fitter, more radiant and full of energy!

**Uwe Karstadt**
Author of 10 bestsellers

---

In our center with more than 20 holistic therapists and more than 20,000 treatments per year, we were able to determine that there are three major hurdles that can significantly block the success of treatment in chronically ill people. These factors are: lack of essential nutrients, exposure to toxic substances and, above all, disorders of the intestinal microbiome.

Especially in connection with the last factor, we, and even more so our patients, are infinitely grateful to Marion Schaatsbergen because she taught us how to spectacularly improve the efficiency of intestinal cleansing. We have understood that the "liberation" of the intestinal mucous membranes from pathogenic biofilms is actually a prerequisite in order to then allow the intestinal barrier to regenerate again and to initially carry out an optimum symbiosis control with prebiotics and probiotics.

Since then we have noticed a quantum leap in our treatment successes. After removing the biofilm beforehand, we saw that our patients with years of migraine issues, auto-immune reactions, depressive moods, chronic fatigue and many other issues could benefit enormously.
For us, Marion is a heroine and I am convinced that the knowledge that she also passes on in this book will make her the same for many other therapists who think holistically.

**Jesse De Groodt**
Osteopath and Lecturer in Integrative Holistic Medicine

Marion Schaatsbergen is a woman of action, a woman who has gained her knowledge from practical experience. The best part is that she shares this knowledge. Today, as readers of her book, we are fortunate to benefit from her experiences, her finds, insights and her incredibly profound knowledge. In this book she tells us everything about health, about the gut and about biofilm (in the gut). Backgrounds, connections, solutions.

I hope that many people will read this book and, with what they learn from it, will begin their journey towards healing and health.

Thank you very much, dear Marion.

**Marlene E Kunold**
Naturopath, Author

# Table of Contents

# Introduction: Your Gut, Your Life

"Health begins in the gut". So said the Ancient Greek physician Hippocrates over 2,500 years ago. Whether you feel good or not is determined in your gut. Even chronic diseases such as rheumatic disorders, depression and type 2 diabetes, which may not seem related to the gut, often do originate there.

The condition of your gut affects how you feel and how you function to such an extent that it is often referred to as the second brain. After all, our gut is much more than just our food digestion factory and supplier of nutrients and energy. Like the brain, it contains a nervous system. Brain and gut communicate directly with one another. When you're anxious, you may feel nauseous as well. This goes both ways. If your bowels are not healthy, they send signals of discomfort to your brain that can affect your mood and behavior. In short, a good bowel condition keeps you comfortable and energetic.

This book is born from a mission: my desire to make the world a healthier place by sharing my knowledge about the gut. As a natural health therapist, I describe how your gut works and what you can do to get and keep it in top shape. *The Gut: Gateway to Health* is based on over 35 years of practical experience in restoring thousands of people's bowels to health and providing education on the subject.

## Toxic surroundings

We may not realize it, but the world we live in is attacking our bodies, and especially our gut, on a daily basis. Even those who eat sensibly, exercise a lot and get plenty of rest can't escape it. The threats we're exposed to are difficult to recognize: invisible pollution in the air, drinking water and food.

Consider, for instance, the air you breathe. People die prematurely each year due to nitrogen dioxide and particulate matter. Even our drinking water, despite strict inspections at drinking water companies, is not as clean as we might think. It can still be contaminated on the way to the tap.

The nutritional value of our food has also deteriorated noticeably in recent decades. A great deal of land has been depleted by intensive agriculture and crops grown on this soil contain fewer minerals. If you add this to the fact that most people don't eat enough fruit and vegetables as it is, we're not ingesting nearly enough minerals and vitamins. Moreover, we spend so much of our time indoors that we don't get enough sunlight and therefore don't produce sufficient vitamin D.

All in all, our bodies – and particularly our intestinal system – are facing some serious challenges. The result? You don't feel as good as you would in an optimum state.

Fortunately, it's not all doom and gloom. Simple and effective solutions are available and I'm happy to share these with you in this book. Once you understand how you can become ill and what the role of your gut is, you already have a head start. And, if you then learn what you can do to cleanse and restore your bowels and with it the body, you're holding the key to your own health.

## Expert experience

My understanding of the gut is not the only reason that prompted me to write this book. As a child, I was very sick due to ruptured appendix, which the family doctor left untreated for three days. As a result, my abdomen became completely inflamed and, even after surgery, I was left with many abdominal complaints. Mainstream medicine had no solution for the abdominal pain I suffered as a child. At the age of fourteen, I met with a naturopath who relieved me of some of the pain. It was a revelation. I was quickly eager to learn more.

At seventeen, I stumbled across a magazine article about the Academie voor Natuurgeneeskunde (Academy for Naturopathy) in Hilversum, The Netherlands. I instantly knew I wanted to study there. Gaining knowledge about natural ways of healing and the prevailing culture, where you were encouraged to be investigative and inquisitive, proved to be right up my alley.

It was a classical education featuring a great deal of knowledge about what health actually entails, with intestinal cleansing as the basis for a healthy body. Due to the knowledge I gained, I started eating more healthily and taking the right supplements. I quickly noticed that my stomach pain was disappearing and my energy level improving.

From then on I was extremely motivated to keep my gut in top condition. To this day, whenever I get an ultrasound of my abdomen, mainstream doctors are always surprised when they observe the mess inflicted by the rupture of my inflamed appendix. “Aren’t you in pain? How are you capable of working?” they’ll ask. They can’t believe that I’m not experiencing any complaints simply because I keep my bowels in top condition.

## A full practice

Thanks to the academy, I embarked on a new life path. Among other things, I went to work for a German producer of homeopathic remedies and herbal extracts as a representative and organizer of training courses for doctors. This proved to be a highly valuable experience. I learned a great deal about the contents of various remedies and the experience doctors had with them in patients.

Using my newly acquired knowledge, I started my own naturopathic practice in 1985 at age 23, in a treatment room at a health food store in Amsterdam. I also gave talks in community centers on ways to feel better using natural remedies. People came to me with a whole range of complaints: intestinal problems, cardiovascular diseases, skin conditions, headaches. My clients felt better after treatment and spread the word. This resulted in a full practice from the very start. Over the years, thousands of clients came to my practice: men, women, the old, the young, the educated, the uneducated and the critically ill as well as people who were still functioning just fine.

## To measure is to know

My hunger for more knowledge about natural healing of the body never went away. Every client is unique, and I wanted to know more about exactly what happens in the body that causes people to become ill. I attended electroacupuncture training, learning to measure the organs and energy and then applying appropriate means – vitamins, minerals and herbs, for example – to get the organs functioning properly again. In my practice, I conducted measurements on clients with my bioresonance device to detect disturbances in the electrical frequencies produced by each organ. The device enables you to measure which organs in the body function optimally and which do not, long before medical procedures can detect it. This allows you to find out which remedies work well, and which do not. I applied it to the gut and this helped me to see, before, during and after intestinal cleansing cures, whether bowel function improved.

In the 1990s, through electroacupuncture, I came into contact with Johan Boswinkel. He was the leading expert on the body's electrical frequencies and had developed his own version of a bioresonance device which allowed him to record the electrical frequencies produced by each human cell more precisely. I was trained by him and started working with his device. This allowed me to measure in my clients, exactly what worked and what did not.

## Harmful biofilm

The basis of my practice was and remained intestinal cleansing. Flushing the bowels with water as a way of cleansing them (colon hydrotherapy) is a well-established practice. In the 1990s, colon hydrotherapy was revived when a machine came on the market that made bowel irrigation more accessible. Through a hose, not only could the water enter through the anus, but the contaminated backwash could also be discharged directly into the sewer. There was no more stench and the client no longer had to run to the bathroom after being flushed. I also used this method to treat people and I could measure the changes with my bioresonance device before, during and after irrigation.

I must have done thousands of those flushes, and yet something bothered me. While the values for the colon soon improved, those for the small intestine barely did. The biofilm, a layer of harmful bacteria that attacks the healthy mucous membrane of the bowels, apparently did not dissolve during the bowel irrigation. I did see progress, but it wasn't enough. People with rheumatoid arthritis, diabetes or bowel issues were therefore required to go on a diet for six weeks every year and undergo bowel irrigation twice a week during this diet. Clients thus spent a lot of time and money on treatment with minimal effect on the small intestine. This prompted me to continue my search for a better bowel cleansing method.

## A clean small intestine

An American colleague informed me about an Asian remedy, one that did effectively target the biofilm in the small intestine. I was skeptical as I had already tried so many different things. By that time I had tested all resources available on the market. First on myself, and when I noticed a positive effect, on clients.

I ordered the Asian product, which contains palm fiber and okra, and started testing it on myself. Two days later, I was quite surprised when a huge string of dirt was released from my intestines. So

my bowels – the bowels of a person who lived a very healthy life, ate only organic produce and did an intestinal cleanse each year – turned out not to be so clean after all. After the treatment, a measurement with the bioresonance device confirmed what had happened. My small intestine was now showing better values, consisting of a normalized pattern of electrical frequencies.
I could hardly sleep for a week from excitement. After all, much of what I had learned about bowel cleansing turned out to be untrue. Existing methods did not sufficiently cleanse the intestines. The only way to restore my sleep was to do something with this new product. The first step was to attend a training course with the manufacturer.

## Complaint free

Once I started working with this remedy on others, their small intestinal values left me stunned. Rather than months of irrigation, clients could now get rid of their biofilm in as little as three to six days. They instantly felt better. After detoxing their bowels, they became fitter, more clear-headed and had fewer cravings for sweets and fats.
Naturopathy is an empirical science. Its effectiveness is proven by good results as compared to the kind of scientific research which is often funded by the pharmaceutical industry. I act based on findings. After all, those who heal are right.
Many clients were completely relieved of their symptoms. Someone with rheumatoid arthritis regained flexible joints after six weeks of detoxification. A client with diabetes no longer needed to inject insulin after the detox. And I can still see the farmer who came into my practice a few years ago, hunched and in pain because his cervical vertebrae were stuck, preventing sufficient blood flow to his brain. With detox treatment and vitamin supplements, a healthy blood supply to his brain was restored and I was able to refer him to a manual therapist or chiropractor for further treatment of his neck pain. (I often work with other practitioners so that a client can address complaints not related to the gut as well.)

## Regular and alternative

If necessary, I also refer to the primary care physician. When dealing with urgent complaints, this is best. Nor am I at all opposed to mainstream medicine. I have benefited from it myself. It saved my life after my appendix burst. And after falling off my horse as a teenager, I naturally went to hospital to receive treatment for my pneumothorax, bruised cervical vertebrae and shattered shoulder. Moreover, if you have cancer, I believe that getting hospital treatment is the way to go. After that, you can start detoxing with a detox therapist to prevent the cancer from coming back.
Conventional medicine and naturopathy complement each other. Regular doctors tend to do the things they are trained to do very well. When dealing with chronic complaints, however, they often don't seem to have the answer. In my experience, by the way, they are the first to admit this. As for chronic complaints, a doctor is only trained to treat the symptoms, while naturopathy addresses the causes.

## Knowledge is everything

The curing of symptoms starts with awareness and knowledge. How does the body work, how does it become ill and what can you do to restore it to health? It's about taking responsibility for your own body. When it comes to staying healthy, there's so much you can do. Gaining knowledge about how your body works is a good first step. Next, it's about effective methods and products for detoxification. Then you must continue to apply the knowledge you've gained in your diet and lifestyle in order to stay healthy after cleansing your bowels.
This book is about how to improve your basic health, even if you have chronic symptoms. When you work on boosting your digestion and intestines, many symptoms will disappear or bother you much less. If you take good care of your body, especially your gut, symptoms will cease to arise and chronic ailments will disappear.

A healthy diet is not enough. You may eat sensibly, but unhealthy intestines are not very good at absorbing nutrients and so prevent your body benefitting from all that wholesome food.
In this book I describe how you can become ill from contaminated intestines and how to effectively cleanse them. The approach I describe can be applied effectively with just a few changes in your lifestyle and a handful of supplements. It's actually much easier than you might think.
Knowledge is everything and so I have personally focused on training and product development in recent years. This is how I intend to spread the extensive knowledge I've gained on how to become healthier, fitter and more energetic. I believe and hope it will bring benefit to many people.

## Investing in health is a choice

A lot of people think of health and becoming ill as a matter of luck or fate, others see it as something they've inherited through genes. In this book you'll read that good health, or the lack of it, is not something that comes about by chance.
As for the human body, at the end of the day what you put into it and what you expose it to largely determine your health. They are cause and effect. Fortunately, many people already understand the importance of making wise decisions such as eating the right diet, getting plenty of exercise and drinking enough water. There's even more you can do to improve your health, however, and it all starts in the gut. Better health is a choice and in order to make that choice you need the right information.
It's also a matter of changing the way you look at things. Improving your health does not come naturally and it's not free. In a way, it's strange that we've come to think of it this way. If you tell the average person their car has to go to the repair shop and they must pay for it, they simply pay. When it comes to the much needed maintenance of the body, however, people are not so sure. This is quite remarkable

considering you spend only 1 to 2 hours a day in your car, and 24 in your body. On the contrary, if you ask people what's most important in life you generally get two answers: love and health. True love obviously cannot be bought, but improved health usually can. This book is about the steps you can take to achieve it, and why it matters.

1

# It All Comes Down to Digestion

*The body is a miracle of ingenuity. The role of the gut has been overlooked for a long time. The gut does far more than nourish your body by digesting food and making nutrients available to your organs. It also determines how you feel and controls your behavior. In that respect, your gut is like a second brain. If you take good care of your gut, your quality of life will improve immensely. So how does this miraculous food-digesting machine work? You'll read more about it in this chapter.*

## Older, not healthier

In our Western society, a large group of people enjoy great prosperity. This is mainly due to the vast amount of knowledge we've accumulated over the centuries. In the areas of nutrition and health, for example, great progress has been made. As a result, most deadly infectious diseases such as the plague and syphilis which killed millions of people in the past, have fortunately disappeared. We know now how these diseases spread and how to effectively control them.

As a result, our living conditions have become considerably more hygienic. Our drinking water is relatively clean, allowing you to drink it worry free. Our household waste is collected, preventing it from ending up in the streets where disease-spreading pests can reach it. The sewers are below ground now, ensuring you don't come into contact with dirty water and feces and get sick as a result. Our food has also become increasingly varied and safer. In most countries, Food Safety Authorities check food offered in stores and restaurants for hygienic quality and the presence of disease-causing bacteria.

With all these improvements in terms of health and hygiene, we live much longer than our ancestors did. In theory, we can live to be 120 years old. However, despite the enormous progress we've made, we rarely do reach 120. In fact, our basic health has improved much less than you might expect. In today's world, we're exposed to all kinds of unhealthy substances through air pollution and the food we eat – think of artificial colorings, aromas, flavorings and pesticide residues.

The fact that we are nonetheless getting older than we used to, is mainly because medical science has enabled doctors to stretch people's lives with medication. This allows us to live longer lives, but does not necessarily improve the quality of our lives. We're not so much getting older, but we're dying more slowly.

If you have acute symptoms, such as a broken leg, appendicitis or cancer, regular health care can help you just fine. However, for chronic ailments such as gastrointestinal problems, heart disease and rheumatic complaints, mainstream health care often doesn't have a solution. Its primary focus is on combating symptoms rather than preventing them by tackling them at the source. This poses a major concern because 6 in 10 Americans suffer from at least one chronic disease, such as heart disease, stroke, cancer, or diabetes. These and other chronic diseases are the leading causes of death and disability in America and they are also a leading driver of health care costs.

Fortunately, there's a lot *you* can do in order to feel fitter, more energized and healthier and to reduce chronic symptoms. The first thing requirement is knowledge of how your body works and the role digestion plays in it.

## Our body is infinitely intelligent

In essence, our body is a highly intelligent machine. It consists of an impressive 30 trillion cells which constantly renew themselves. This is a miracle in itself since we, as humans, originate from a single fertilized egg cell. It takes us a while to finish growing, but even at 25 – the age at which we are roughly mature – our cells continue to renew themselves. Each cell type has its own lifespan. White blood cells, which help fight infections, live for just a few hours. Some nerve cells, on the other hand, last a lifetime.

The cell is the smallest entity of the human body that can live independently. You can continue to grow one in a glass lab dish. Cells also play an important role in your digestive system. Your gut processes nutrients to be absorbed by the bloodstream where they enter your cells. Each cell contains a large number of mitochondria, the energy factories. They convert the digested nutrients into energy, allowing the cell to function and renew itself when necessary.

Each cell type has a unique purpose. Skin cells protect our bodies from undesirable external influences. Eye cells allow us to see the world around us. Bone cells keep our skeleton strong. Cells are aware of their tasks within our body because their nucleus contains DNA. All cells receive roughly the same nutrients through your blood, but the cell nucleus then determines what the cell does with them.

The cells constantly renew themselves, causing almost your entire body to renew several times during your lifetime. Naturally, it can only succeed if your digestive system works properly. Only then will all those cells that need renewing receive the right nutrients.

## Oxygen and fuel

The intelligent machine that is your body, which is made up of trillions of cells, requires two things to function: oxygen and fuel. Oxygen is supplied to your body through breathing, which happens more or less automatically. All you need is a pair of functioning lungs and air that's not too polluted. The oxygen your body needs, can be absorbed directly by the lungs.

For fuel, your body uses food. For it to be of any use, this shouldn't be too polluted either. Part of the pollutants are filtered out of your food by your intestines, liver and kidneys. What remains often goes unnoticed by your body in the short term. Even if you're eating extremely unhealthy foods, your body just keeps on living. A lack of the right minerals can cause certain enzyme processes in the body to malfunction. Instead of healthy minerals, the body then starts using the heavy metals that we all ingest, for example through our food. This is obviously bad for you in the long run, but for now, your body makes sure you stay alive.

Partly because so many of us are cremated these days, we were found to have many more pollutants in our bodies lately due to unhealthy living conditions. About 50 years ago, the deceased were cremated at 752 degrees Fahrenheit. Now, most ovens are set much hotter, otherwise the bodies don't turn to ashes properly. Most likely, this has to do with the chemicals and heavy metals in those bodies.

Apart from "using" heavy metals, your body has more clever tricks to keep you alive in adverse conditions. If you can't get rid of all the toxins through your intestines, kidneys and liver, your body tries to limit the damage by excreting toxins through our so called "third kidney": the skin. This causes the acidity of the skin to deteriorate, making it a breeding ground for pathogenic bacteria, which can cause infections and rashes.

Pollution is obviously disastrous in the long run. Too many toxins enter your body and your cells become polluted, which means they can no longer absorb enough oxygen. This can eventually develop into a fatal illness. Before then, your intestines will make every effort to keep you well supplied with nutrients and thus alive. To do so, they have their work cut out for them during digestion.

## Your clever digestive system

Oxygen is absorbed relatively easily by the body, but food needs a lot of processing before your body can use it. Let's take a closer look at how your clever digestive system works. Imagine a plate with boiled potatoes, a piece of chicken breast and some carrots. You can already smell the spiced chicken as you take your seat at the table. You pick up your knife, cut off a piece of chicken and take a bite. And with that, the conversion of food into nutrients for your body has started.

The digestive system takes up a large part of your body. This is a first indication of how vitally important it is. It is a highly ingenious system, consisting of multiple organs that all play their part in breaking down your food into nutrients and fuel.

Figure 1.1 provides an overview of the entire digestive system. It reveals how many organs are involved and demonstrates the phases in which your food is broken down until your body can use that potato, chicken or carrot as building material or energy source. In your mouth, the food is chewed and mixed with saliva, breaking it down into small pieces and "pre-soaking" it. The esophagus carries the chewed food to the stomach, where it enters the second phase of digestion. The food is kneaded further and gastric juices are added.

The third, and most crucial, phase takes place in the gut. That's where the most radical digestion occurs, after which it is absorbed by the body. At that point, the indigestible remains of your potatoes, chicken and carrots have turned into an unrecognizable mush, that is stripped of water and salt in the colon. What remains eventually ends up in the toilet.

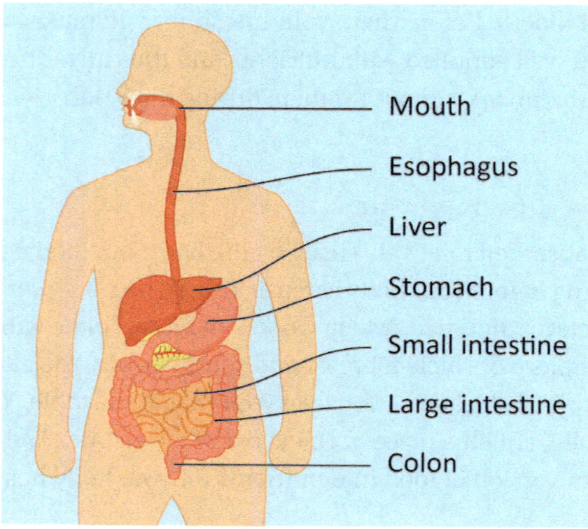


Figure 1.1 The elements of our digestive system

To achieve a thorough understanding of why digestion plays such a vital role in your physical well-being and in your overall health, we'll take a closer look at the role of each organ in the digestive system. This will already reveal a little about what can go wrong and how you can affect your own digestion and well-being.

### *The mouth*

One thing about digestion not many people know, is that it starts before any food even enters the mouth. As soon as you see or smell those potatoes, chicken and carrots, a signal already goes to your brain: "produce saliva," causing your mouth to water. Sometimes, you can even feel the sudden salivation as a stinging sensation in the back of your mouth, near the end of your jaws. You produce as much as a quarter gallon of saliva that way each day.

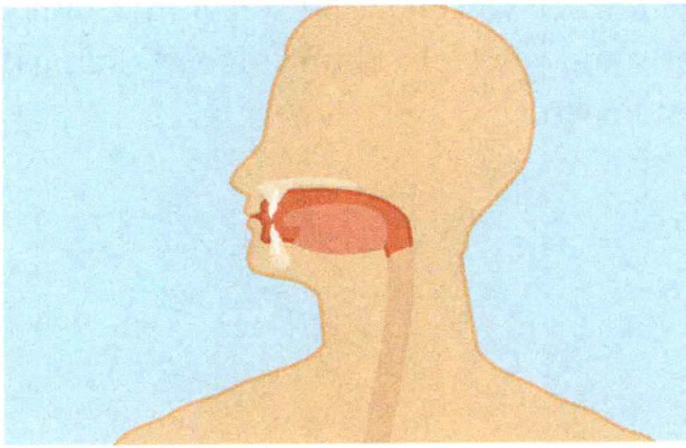

Figure 1.2 The mouth: where digestion starts

Once you've taken a bite, your molars grind the potatoes, chicken and carrots. Proper chewing is necessary for the mouth to effectively perform its digestive task.

For proper digestion, your potatoes, chicken and carrots are mixed with saliva in your mouth. Saliva contains the enzymes amylase and lysozyme. These enzymes are created by your body and enable or speed up chemical reactions. They don't consume any energy. Amylase "cuts" carbohydrates, which are found in your potatoes and carrots, into tiny pieces. Chicken doesn't contain any carbohydrates, it's merely ground into small pieces in your mouth. Lysozyme attacks the unhealthy bacteria in your food and kills some of them already.

Your tongue then pushes the finely ground potatoes, chicken and carrots down your esophagus. You can positively influence this first stage of digestion by choosing healthy foods and chewing them properly. A healthy diet is vital in order to be left with good building materials and energy sources after digestion.

### *The esophagus*

The finely ground potatoes, chicken and carrots mixed with saliva are now in your esophagus. This is a straight transport pipe of about 10 inches long, which ends at the same height as your armpit. You can clearly feel it when you choke on something, or if you haven't chewed properly and you feel a chunk of food sliding down slowly towards your stomach.

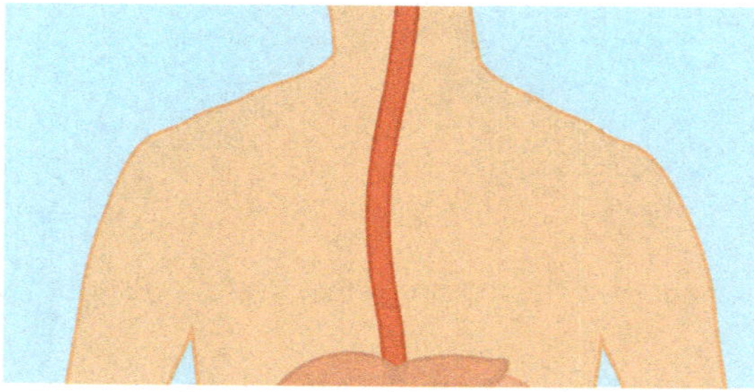

Figure 1.3 The esophagus: food transport pipe

Through the esophagus, the ground food is transported from mouth to stomach. Your food doesn't just simply drop down. Muscles in the esophagus pull together and relax, thus allowing the ground food to enter the stomach slowly. To ensure that the food glides smoothly, the esophagus produces mucus as a kind of lubricant.

At the top of the stomach is a small muscle, the stomach sphincter, which opens to allow food coming from the esophagus down into the stomach. Then it closes again, preventing the food and stomach juice from flowing back to the esophagus. Gastric juice is incredibly acidic, it could damage the esophageal wall. Once the stomach has produced enough gastric acid, the stomach's sphincter receives a signal to close and the stomach can start its task.

### *The stomach*

The ground and soaked potatoes, chicken and carrots have now arrived in the stomach. This elastic, pear shaped sack of about 12 inches long is located at the top of the abdomen, just below the diaphragm and to the left of the center. It is well protected there, but if you were to fall with your bike and the wheel hits your belly, you'd feel pain in your stomach area.
With so much food to digest each day, the stomach is very flexible. When fully expanded it can hold up to a gallon of water.

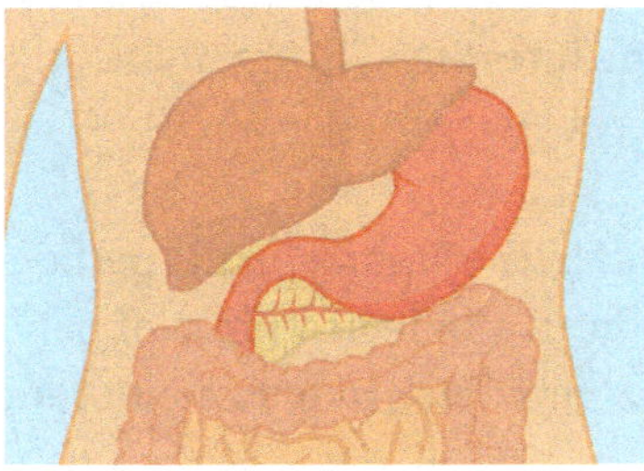

Figure 1.4 The stomach: a powerful digestive muscle

The stomach is not always ready to receive food. When you're stressed, you can have the feeling that you simply cannot swallow another bite. Stress is an indication that your attention is needed elsewhere: a complicated traffic situation, an injured child or an exam. Your stomach tightens and your body allows more blood to go to your brain so you can take appropriate action. This is another example of your body's intelligence, it adapts to your specific circumstances.

The stomach is not only flexible and sensitive, but also very strong. The stomach wall is about 0.2 inches thick and consists of three different layers of tissue. The stomach produces as much as 6.5 cups of gastric juice every 24 hours. This is mixed with the pieces of potato, chicken and carrot to further process them.

The gastric juice is able to break down food because it contains enzymes and hydrochloric acid. The enzymes in your stomach break down the carbohydrates from your potatoes and carrots, while hydrochloric acid pre-digests proteins. The proteins are broken down further during a later stage of digestion.

The stomach needs about three hours for all this, longer if you've eaten fatty foods. It takes more time to digest French fries and chicken kebabs, for example, than boiled potatoes and chicken breast. At the far end of the stomach is another sphincter, which provides access to the intestines. In small bits, the stomach passes on the food it has digested.

The hydrochloric acid in the stomach kills pathogenic bacteria. It's so strong that it can burn a hole in a piece of paper. The stomach wall is protected by a very thick mucus membrane.

When stomach acid travels up towards the throat (acid reflux) this can cause a burning sensation in the chest (heartburn). Many people think acid reflux is caused by an overproduction of stomach acid, while, in fact, the opposite is true. Acid reflux is a symptom of too little stomach acid rather than too much. Your stomach sphincter doesn't close until you have produced enough stomach acid, which is when the brain receives a signal to close. Acid reflux occurs as a result of a poorly closing sphincter muscle at the top of the stomach, allowing the contents to move upward.

The fact that the stomach is highly acidic is imperative for the overall digestion of food. If you drink water during meals, you're basically diluting stomach acid, causing the food to be digested less well. Therefore, it's better not to drink for half an hour before or after a meal. Other than that, drinking plenty of fluids is highly beneficial. Cold drinks, however, affect your digestion in a negative way. They chill your stomach, slowing down the functioning of the enzymes there and in your gut – and thus the digestion of your food. Enzymes, in fact, are at their best at a temperature between 96.8 and 100.4 degrees Fahrenheit. If you cool your digestive system too much with cold drinks, it will be a while before it again works as well as it should. Lukewarm water and herbal teas are therefore highly recommended.

After the stomach has processed your food, it passes the partially digested food pulp on to the small intestine for the next stage of digestion.

### *The duodenum*

The first part of the small intestine, the duodenum, was named by the Greek physician Herophilus (335-280 B.C.). In Latin, the term "duodenum" means 12 fingers, which is roughly the length of the duodenum (8 to 10 inches). This type of fingerbreadth measurement was used in the early days of surgery.

The first thing the duodenum does with the chicken-potato-carrot soup it receives from the stomach is to make it less acidic. This is essential for the digestive enzymes in the duodenum to perform their task properly. The intestinal wall contains less mucus than the stomach wall and is therefore less protected against hydrochloric acid brought with it by the partially digested food mush.

In the duodenum, the pancreas and gallbladder add digestive juices, which process the food further. The pancreas is located on the left side of the upper abdomen, just in front of the spine and produces enzymes that break down carbohydrates, proteins and fat. It also releases hormones to balance blood sugar levels.

The liver is located on the right side of your body, below the ribs, and is responsible for producing bile. This bitter, acid, green liquid is stored in the gallbladder, which lies below the liver, until the body needs it. The moment fats enter your stomach and gut, the gallbladder receives a signal to inject bile fluid into the gut to break them down. Our bodies are supposed to produce as much as a quarter gallon of this vital fluid every 24 hours, which not only breaks down fats, but also enhances proper bowel movements. Regrettably, due to the modern human diet, the amount of bile fluid we produce has become a lot less, with dire consequences.

After being processed with digestive juices, your potatoes, chicken and carrots have been converted into valuable nutrients which are absorbed by your body into the blood stream through the intestinal wall. Your meal is now beyond recognition. Its nutrients enter the blood stream and are further transported to the body's cells, which can then use them as fuel.

### *The small intestine*

The small intestine is about 16 to 20 feet long and the intestinal wall covers a total area of 1600 to 2200 square feet – the size of a tennis court. The reason it can even fit in your belly is because it's folded like a harmonica. Your intestinal wall has protrusions everywhere that look like fingers, creating a large surface area that can deliver nutrients to the blood vessels around the small intestine.

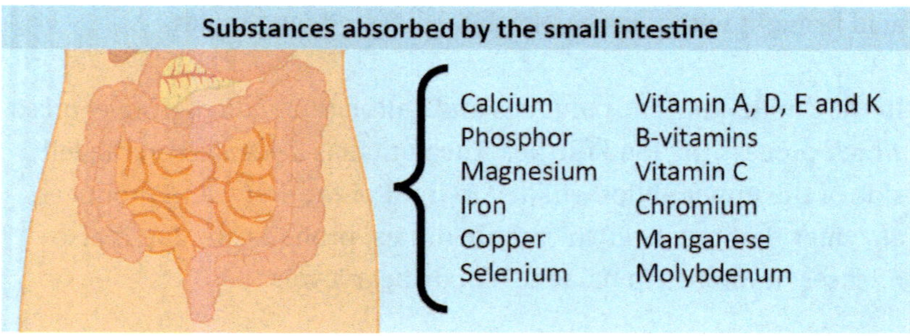


Figure 1.5 The small intestine: center of digestion

If you look at the enormous size of the small intestine, it's clear this is where the most important part of digestion happens. The importance of this organ is also reflected in the fact that, through the intestinal wall, a large number of proteins, carbohydrates, fats and minerals are absorbed by the blood and transported to the rest of the body.

We have about 30 trillion body cells and 38 trillion bacteria. The bacteria in your body are of vital importance, you can think of them as little soldiers. Not only do they help with digestion and produce vitamin K and certain B vitamins, but they also boost your immune system, increasing your body's natural resistance. They produce hydrogen peroxide, for example, which suppresses pathogenic bacteria and pathogenic organisms such as yeasts and fungi.

The gut is home to billions of bacteria: good and bad. All those bacteria combined are called the "gut flora" or "microbiome". Each person has their own specific microbiome. In healthy people, the good bacteria keep the bad ones in check. Having a healthy gut flora is vital for digestion. You can influence the composition of your gut flora by eating the right food. Eating lots of processed foods with added sugars and chemicals gives the bad bacteria in your gut a chance to multiply quickly. In other words, poor nutrition means your body must put in extra effort to repair the damage.

Food is not the only thing that affects your gut flora. Antibiotics to treat, say, a bladder infection can kill the good gut bacteria along with the bad ones that caused the infection. Fortunately, it is quite possible to replenish the number of good bacteria in the gut when a deficiency occurs after a period of stress, poor nutrition, antibiotic treatments or surgery. Specific products exist for this purpose. I'll discuss them in more detail in Chapter 6.

In the gut, food from the stomach which has been transformed into a kind of thick soup through the addition of gastric juice is broken down further. The useful components are supplied to the blood through the intestinal wall. If your gut isn't working properly, your body will not be able to absorb enough nutrients. This also prevents your immune system from producing sufficient antibodies, as well as failing to produce several types of vitamin altogether. Your body will start underperforming as a result. You'll feel tired or less energized, and become more susceptible to diseases including chronic ones.

### *The lower part of the small intestine*

The lower part of the small intestine is where the digestion is finalized. The proteins and fats from your chicken, the carbohydrates from your potatoes and carrots, and the vitamins and minerals are further digested with the help of bile fluid and the enzymes from the pancreas. Here, many beneficial nutrients – such as vitamin B12 – are absorbed into your body. This demonstrates the importance of a well-functioning small intestine. You can eat as sensibly as you like and if your small intestine doesn't absorb nutrients properly, you will rapidly build up deficiencies.

Once the nutrients are absorbed by your intestinal wall, they are transported to your liver by your blood and lymph fluid. The liver has several purposes. It produces the bile fluid your gut uses to break down fat, and it converts nutrients from the gut into useful substances that can be absorbed by the body's cells and used as building materials and energy sources. The liver also eliminates toxins, such as alcohol, chemical compounds and heavy metals.

### *The large intestine*

The food particles that remain enter the last part of the digestive system: the large intestine, also called the colon. It is over three feet long and shaped like an upside-down letter U.

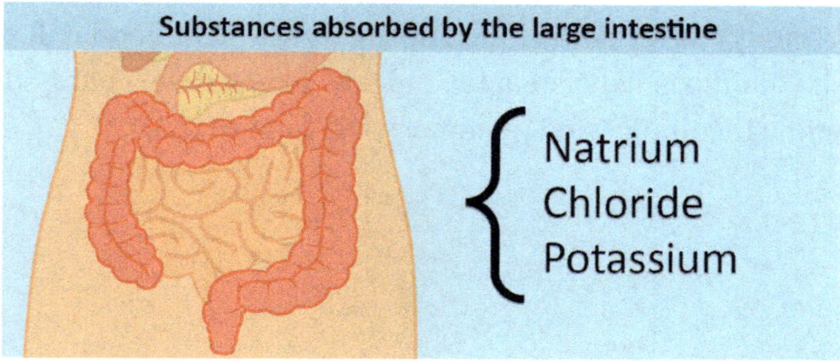


Figure 1.6 The large intestine: fighter of bad bacteria

While the job of the small intestine is mainly to digest food, that of the large intestine is mainly to fight bad bacteria, strengthen your immune system and absorb water and salt from the food mash. No more digestion takes place here. The good bacteria in the large intestine also produce vitamins which are absorbed by the mucous membrane.

One component of the large intestine is the appendix, which was long thought to be useless. In the early 20th century, however, scientists discovered that the appendix is packed with white blood cells, which support the immune system. So it turns out it's rather useful after all!

### *The rectum*

After the last fluid and salt are extracted by the large intestine, the remainder of your food travels to the rectum. Approximately 24 to 48 hours after you took that first bite of chicken, your plate of food has become a brown mush of indigestible residue: poop. When the rectum is full, your brain receives a signal: "go to the bathroom". The large intestine makes pendulum movements to relieve you of the indigestible parts of your food.

Exactly how long it takes to digest your food depends on what you've eaten and the state of your gut flora. Fatty foods are digested more slowly, and if you drink too much during meals, your food will pass through your digestive system too quickly. In any case, your body will excrete the undigested remains in the form of feces.

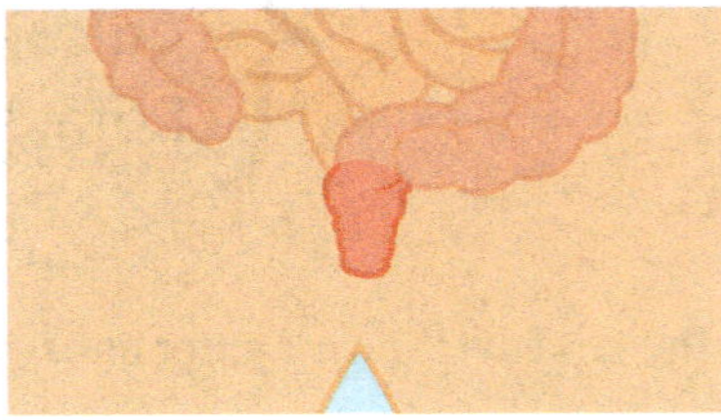

Figure 1.7 The rectum: outlet of the colon

## What can you learn from poop?

Poop is the residual product of the potatoes, chicken and carrots that were on your plate one or two days earlier. Many factors determine what that residue ultimately looks like and how quickly, or slowly, it comes out. Taking a glance at your poop after a visit to the bathroom can give you information about the state of your digestion and gut.

The pooping process and good poop have the following characteristics:

- Your poop comes once or twice a day at a set time.
- It's painless. If you're experiencing pain, there are certain abnormalities in the rectum.
- Cramps, mucus and excessive gas are not a normal part of it. This could indicate poor digestion or an infection.
- Your poop is shaped like a brown sausage.
- It doesn't smell excessively. If it does, the food is not adequately digested or there are too many bad bacteria in the gut.
- It doesn't stick to the toilet bowl. If it does, it contains too many undigested fats.

- It does not contain undigested bits. That would indicate a lack of digestive enzymes in the gut.
- Your poop doesn't float. If it does, it could indicate gas or excess undigested fats in the stool.
- There certainly shouldn't be any blood in your stool. If that's the case, you should see a doctor.

## True health

How you feel and what your poop looks like tells you something about the state of your health, but how do you know whether you're truly healthy? After all, health does not consist of the absence of complaints and symptoms. There are many people with unhealthy bowels who experience no symptoms at all. In fact, being truly ill is preceded by a phase in which, although the body is underperforming, we don't yet experience any serious symptoms. However, this may be a preliminary stage of symptoms and diseases that develop later on, such as candida or other fungal infections, joint pain, lowered immunity, weight gain and eventually diabetes, multiple sclerosis, cardiovascular disease or cancer.

Many illnesses, even if they don't seem to be directly related to digestion, are a result of damage to the body caused by an unhealthy environment, lifestyle and diet. The body is overburdened by far more harmful substances than it can handle. The number of diseases directly related to the stomach, liver and intestines alone is shockingly high. According to a study by the US National Library of Medicine from 2015 there were more than 54.5 million ambulatory visits per year with a primary diagnosis for a gastrointestinal disease, 3.0 million hospital admissions, and 540,500 all-cause 30-day readmissions. 60 to 70 million people suffer from stomach complaints.

So, being healthy is not the same as being complaint free. Being healthy means all organs and organ systems functioning at their optimum. This is the case when all cells receive the right nutrients and burn those substances completely, without any waste products. In this day and age, however, this mechanism is severely compromised. We're exposed to thousands of substances, such as dyes, food aromas and flavors, toxic building materials or heavy metals that pollute the air, every day. Even if you were to live at the North Pole, you couldn't escape this pollution.

If you want to live a longer and, more importantly, healthier life, the most important thing you can do is burden your body less with waste products. A healthy diet, plenty of exercise and enough rest are key. Sadly though, because we live in such a polluted world, that's not enough. Fortunately, there are a number of easy-to-implement steps available to reduce the burden on your body: colon cleansing, drinking purified water and taking vitamins the body can easily absorb. I'll discuss these further in Chapters 4, 5 and 6.

## The gut: your second brain

There is yet another reason why your gut deserves your attention. A common belief is that the brain controls the gut, setting the bowels in motion. In other words, a one-way street. Indeed, hundreds of millions of neurons (nerve cells) connect the brain to the gut's nervous system. In that way, the brain steers digestion.

Very few people, however, are aware of the fact that our gut is actually made up of the same type of cells as the brain. Gut bacteria produce neurotransmitters: signaling molecules that can control the brain. These substances determine whether we feel happy or depressed, how we digest our food, how we experience pain, how our lungs function and how we sleep. Whether you shy away from, or welcome a change is determined in part by what happens in your gut. Negative emotions, such as depression and anxiety, can also be caused by the state of your gut. Our gut shapes our lives more than we think. It co-manages our body which is why it is referred to as our "second brain".

In short, the connection between brain and gut is definitely a two-way street. Your gut is incredibly important and largely determines your overall health and how you feel and behave. The fact that our gut is often in such bad shape due to pollution is worrisome. The causes and effects of this intestinal pollution are discussed in the next chapter.

## Summary

**Discover your gut: energy factory, purifier and second brain**
Your gut makes up a large part of your body and is incredibly important. It performs multiple tasks. It's an energy factory. Anything you eat is converted into nutrients, which your body then uses as building materials or fuel.

It's also a purification system. It removes toxins and harmful substances from your food 24/7, and keeps you from collapsing, even if you don't eat particularly healthily and live in an area that is polluted.

Finally, the gut also serves as your body's second brain. Through neurotransmitters it controls your brain, thus determining how you feel and influencing the choices you make. Positive emotions, as well as depression or anxiety, can be caused by the state of your gut. If you want to feel happy and energetic, it's important to take good care of your gut.

2

# The Danger of a Polluted Gut

*In chapter 1, we followed the journey of one meal through your body and seen the clever working of our digestive system. Up to the first half of the 20th century, the process of digestion rarely presented any major issues. Due to increased environmental pollution however, our digestive systems have become overloaded. These toxins have a huge impact on the functioning of our gut and can end up causing all kinds of complaints. In other words, pollution is affecting our health. This book is about solutions, but it's also important to address the possible causes. Knowledge of this will give you an even better understanding of the task ahead.*

## Pollution affects everyone

We are currently facing a global health crisis. Environmental pollution is the main culprit. According to the European Chemicals Agency, which registers chemicals and determines their authorization, there are over 171,000 officially authorized chemicals on the European market. About 2,000 new chemicals are added each year, according to the U.S. Department of Health. For most of these chemicals it is not clear whether they are actually safe for humans (United Nations Environmental Program). Mid-2019, the 180 countries affiliated with the United Nations therefore decided to ban

4,000 chemicals that were used in things like non-stick pans, carpet, paper and extinguishing foam.

Whether you find yourself in New York, Nairobi, Paris or Perth, air quality is far from optimum in many parts of the world. Traffic, industry, intensive livestock farming, shipping, aviation and construction release nitrogen oxide and particulate matter into the air.

The quality of drinking water in the Western world is considered to be satisfactory by governments. Drinking water companies do indeed remove the fertilizers and pesticides, heavy metals and chemicals that have entered our water. However, water quality controllers discover new contaminants, such as pharmaceutical and drug residues, in drinking water sources all the time. Moreover, a growing number of microplastics from the chemical industry enter our water and heavy rains cause sewage overflows which also threaten water quality.

bear in mind too that water companies cannot prevent all pollution, such as excessive lead concentrations in tap water due to old lead plumbing. The Drinking Water Infrastructure Needs Survey and Assessment, conducted in 2021 as part of requirements under the Safe Drinking Water Act, looked at more than 3,600 public water systems across the country and its territories. Based on those results, EPA officials estimate that there are roughly 9.2 million lead service lines in the US.

A PNAS report states that in 2015, 9 percent of community water systems in their study sample violated health-based water quality standards, affecting nearly 21 million people. During each of the past 34 years, 9 to 45 million people were affected, representing 4 to 28 percent of the US population.

Our soil is also contaminated with heavy metals and toxic chemicals. Heavy metals are native to nature, but they are now used on a huge scale in many manufacturing processes causing them to end up in unnaturally high concentrations in our soil, water and food. As a result, we're exposed to more heavy metals now than our ancestors were at the beginning of the 20th century. It is much more than our bodies can handle.

Synthetic chemicals are a relatively new phenomenon. In the 1940s and 1950s, the farming and food industries started using these chemicals to make crops grow faster and food last longer. Through the soil, these substances also find their way into plants and animals and thus into our food.

Some of the most toxic chemicals, such as DDT, have been banned over time. Research indicates, however, that DDT is still present in our bodies. What many people don't know is that these toxins are causing the rise in the global prevalence of excess weight and obesity. They seriously interfere with hormonal functions. More than half of our population is already struggling with moderate or severe obesity. Not surprisingly, the statistics showing the increase in chemical pollution in our environment follow the same trend as the graphs showing the growth of obesity.

The pollution that enters our body is stored in adipose tissue. There, it disrupts fat metabolism and our natural weight regulation. In other words, many people are gaining weight not because they're eating too much, but because the contaminants in their food upset their weight balance.

You don't have to be overweight to worry about pollution entering your body through the lungs, skin, food and drinking water. Everyone is affected.

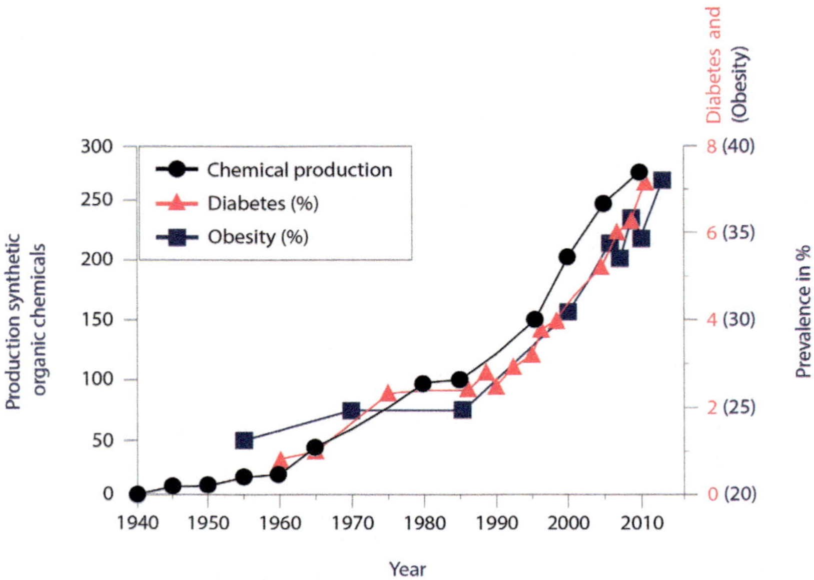


Figure 2.1 Korean researchers have shown that there is a direct link between the increasing production of chemicals and the increase in diabetes and obesity. Source: Lee, 2018.

As a result, our body has to work extremely hard to get rid of all the junk it absorbs every day and to combat its negative effects. One way it does this is by neutralizing toxins with vitamins. Our need for vitamins and other healthy nutrients has therefore skyrocketed since the 1940s. After all, we need more of them to combat the pollution in our bodies.

## Dietary deficiencies

At the same time, another unfavorable development can be observed. Authoritative sources such as the Department of Agriculture report that research shows a decrease in the nutritional value of fruits and vegetables in recent decades. Much of the world's farmland has been depleted. As a result, the amount of

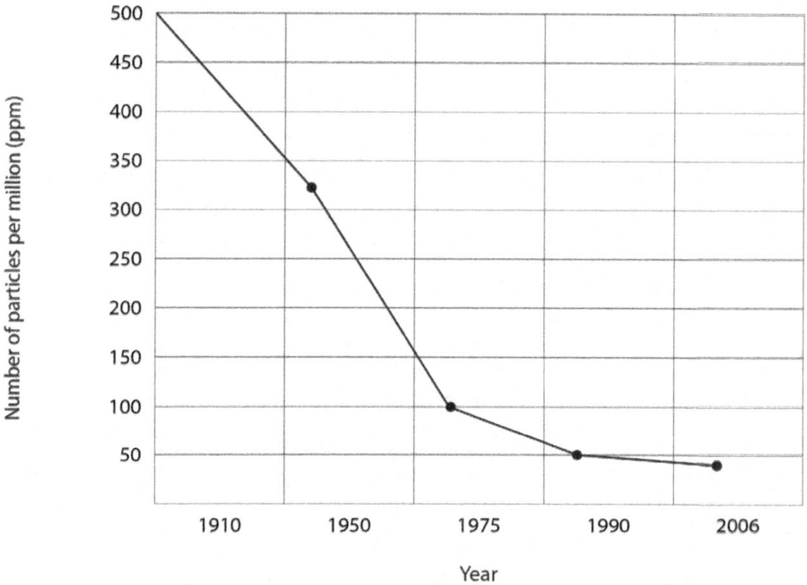


Figure 2.2 Over a century, the amount of minerals in farmland has declined extremely. Source: United States Department of Agriculture (USDA).

minerals in the soil has dropped at an alarming rate over the last century. Farmers try to counteract this by using fertilizers, but that's no substitute for the rich and varied mineral palette in healthy farmland.

And there's more. Fruits and vegetables are often selected purely on appearance – nice and big, for example – and not on nutritional value. On top of that, fruit is often picked unripe, resulting in a lower vitamin content than when harvested ripe. The bottom line is that fruits and vegetables contain fewer minerals and vitamins than they used to.

To make matters worse, there are several chemical weeds and fungicides in circulation, such as the controversial Roundup with the active ingredient glyphosate. These products are capable of killing all bacteria in the soil, including the beneficial bacteria that provide the soil with mineral-rich humus. We are now finding traces of glyphosate throughout the earth's crust, in all the world's water and in all life on earth. Aside from its toxicity to humans, it indirectly reduces the plants' ability to absorb minerals. Fertilizer won't solve all these issues overnight. In any event, it contains only a fraction of the nearly one hundred necessary soil minerals.

In short, pollution and deterioration are converting agricultural and horticultural land into a breeding ground which is far too meager for our food, while that same pollution is actually increasing our need for valuable nutrients. On top of that, CDC has found that only 1 in 10 adults in the US eat enough fruit and vegetables, which means that 9 in 10 adults are rapidly becoming deficient in minerals and vitamins such as B12, B6 and folic acid. Worse, because we spend a lot of our time indoors where we don't get enough sunlight, we don't produce the necessary amount of vitamin D we need.

You don't have to be an expert to figure out that all these developments are compromising your health. Even if you're eating healthily and organically, you're very likely to have deficiencies. Organic food is certainly healthier than industrially produced food, because it's less polluted and has a higher nutritional value. Yet organically grown vegetables still contain insufficient minerals and it's nearly impossible to grow anything glyphosate free – even if the farmer isn't using it – because the pesticide has spread throughout the atmosphere.

## Health risks from radiation

There's another important component to consider when it comes to the burden on your body: electromagnetic radiation from cell phones, Wi-Fi, smart meters and baby monitors and more. Some scientists believe that the existing standards for the permissible electromagnetic fields from these devices are not stringent enough. In fact, studies show that electromagnetic fields affect humans and animals. They pose a greater risk of cancer, damage to our DNA, structural and functional changes in our reproductive system and neurological disorders. In 2015, an international group of more than 200 researchers working on the effects of electromagnetic fields made an appeal to the United Nations. They advocated for measures to counteract exposure and for more research into the risks of electromagnetic radiation, especially in children. From this perspective, you can understand the concerns regarding the introduction of the 5G network whose effects have not been properly studied.

## Abundance of intestinal issues

These forms of pollution affect people everywhere. Almost everyone suffers from an acidified gut environment. Due to this, our cells cannot absorb enough healthy substances. This causes fatigue and a lack of energy in the short term, and chronic diseases – such as diabetes, intestinal diseases, cardiovascular diseases, rheumatism and stomach and liver issues – in the longer term. Chronic disease rates are expected to rise due to unhealthy lifestyles.
Research suggests that many common diseases of affluence in the rich West – such as cancer, hormonal disorders, lack of energy, chronic fatigue, sexual issues, immune disorders and heart disease – can be linked to, or caused by, chemical toxins and pollution.

Chronic illnesses, however, are just the tip of the iceberg when it comes to conditions related to gut pollution. 70 percent of your immunity to disease originates from the gut. Thus, a weakened gut results in weakened immunity, causing all sorts of health issues. In the next chapter, I will discuss the common diseases that are caused by intestinal pollution.

**Pain caused by a toxin ridden body**
Cattle farmer Henry came to me at age 52 with severe rheumatic complaints. His body was stiff, and he had trouble moving around. He had been taking very strong medication, including methotrexate, for his stiffness and pain for over a decade. While this medicine inhibits (rheumatic) inflammation, it also hinders the production of healthy cells in places like the gut. The anti-rheumatic drug was thus also affecting the functioning of his intestines. As a result, not only was he dealing with rheumatic complaints, but he also had low energy levels and suffered from obesity. Not surprisingly, he expressed dissatisfaction with his overall health.

A detoxification cure, supplemented with additional vitamins and minerals to regain his strength, greatly boosted his overall health. His energy levels improved, he was able to move around better again, and he lost weight. The toxins had been removed from his body, which also meant the inflammation in his joints diminished and the rheumatism had less chance. As a result, he barely experienced any more pain.

## Future generations pay the price

The next generation is going to pay the price for all the junk that's entering our bodies, as the health consequences will hit them harder. Throughout their lives, they'll face higher health care bills. After all, not only are children more sensitive to the effects of electromagnetic radiation, they are also more affected by the polluted environment. Their brains and immune systems have not yet matured, so their bodies are less able to cope with the effects of pollution.

Moreover, children are not just affected by polluted air, water and food, but also through our vaccination program. Many vaccines designed to protect children from disease contain toxins such as mercury.

Research from late 2019 (Utrecht University's Faculty of Veterinary Medicine) has shown that mothers also pass toxins from their own bodies on to their (unborn) babies through the amniotic fluid and breast milk. These artificial chemicals interfere with hormonal regulation and can lead to cancer, diabetes, obesity and other developmental, reproductive and neurological issues that can occur long after birth. The very thing nature designed to nourish and protect unborn and newborn babies – amniotic fluid and breast mil –, has sadly also become a source of illness.

Until recently, the placenta was thought to provide a barrier against pollutants. New findings have shown that those substances are passed through the amniotic fluid. Babies also ingest toxins through breast milk. As a result, newborns often start their lives with quite a bit of clutter in their bodies. On top of that comes the pollution we're all exposed to every day through the air, water and food.
To make matters worse, children are more sensitive to chemical damage than adults, damage which they then pass on to their children. And there's more. Contamination is not limited to amniotic fluid and breast milk, semen is also compromised.

## Information can protect you

It is certainly not my intention to burden you with all this information. Mainly I want you to understand the gravity of the problem. After all, being well informed is one of the greatest safeguards we could possibly hope for. With the right information, you can protect yourself better from the effects of bodily contamination. There is still a very real possibility of living a good and healthy life amidst all these chemicals and pollution. I'll tell you how in Chapters 4 and 5.

The most important first step is to analyze the problem and its effects on your body and especially in the gut. What happens in your gut as a result of all that pollution? And how does that lead to a phenomenon that most people have never heard of, but that we all suffer from: biofilm?

## Pollution stimulates harmful bacterial growth

In the previous chapter, you read that the gut is home to billions of bacteria. In a healthy gut, the good and bad bacteria balance each other out. In a polluted gut, however, the intestinal environment becomes acidified. This completely disrupts the balance. Harmful bacteria thrive in an acidic environment. They continue to grow profusely, while the good bacteria cannot cope. If these good bacteria were killed, the outcome would be catastrophic. After all, they are supposed to break down the carrots, potatoes and chicken breast, allowing the nutrients to pass through your intestinal wall and reach your cells via the blood. The blood would then put those nutrients to good use, enabling you to be that energized, well-functioning human being you're meant to be. The pollution entering your body obstructs this healthy course of action.

The fact that harmful bacteria can multiply exponentially in a polluted and acidified environment poses another major problem. Those bacteria have the nasty trait of creating a tough and impenetrable mucus layer around themselves. We call this "biofilm" – the key topic of this book.

Good bacteria don't have such a tough layer of mucus and that's exactly what makes them so vulnerable. The more acidic the environment, the stronger the biofilm becomes, and the harder it is for the good bacteria to keep the bad ones in check.

Biofilm also uses the heavy metals that enter your body to further strengthen itself. Unhealthy guests such as viruses and fungi are also welcomed and absorbed by it. This uncontrolled growth of biofilm can only end in mayhem.

## The harmful biofilm

What exactly is this so called biofilm? It's nothing more than a thin and transparent layer of mucus, invisible to the naked eye. Even the doctor who's examining your colon during a colonoscopy with a camera cannot see it. That harmful biofilm is definitely there however.

The biofilm forms an impermeable layer and protects the harmful bacteria, causing them to become untouchable to the immune system and any kind of treatment. This makes it nearly impossible to fight them, either by natural means or with antibiotics. As a result, the body is burdened with harmful bacteria it can no longer control, making it harder for the good bacteria to survive.

Unfortunately, this isn't the only problem caused by biofilm. It also irritates the intestinal wall by adhering to it. The natural intestinal mucosa dries out, causing the wall to lose its natural protective layer. The cells in the intestinal wall are damaged and it becomes slightly inflamed. You won't feel or notice this in the short term, but it can be disastrous for your health in the long run.

After reading this, you might still think that the biofilm in your gut probably isn't that bad or that it's a rare phenomenon that doesn't affect everyone. Some doctors, in fact, still claim there's no biofilm in the gut.

Its existence, however, has been scientifically proven, as well as the fact that biofilm in the gut can cause major problems. It can lead to serious intestinal diseases and indirectly causes malfunction elsewhere in the body, for example those we might call "modern diseases of affluence". More on that in the next chapter.

## Types of biofilm

It is important to note that the human body has many types of biofilm. It's a part of life. Wherever there are mucous membranes in your body, you'll find biofilm. It's in the sinuses, ears, mouth, throat, eyes, ureters, vagina, intestinal walls and even in our wounds. There's at least one type of biofilm we all know: dental plaque. Of plaque, we know that it's particularly harmful. You have to fight it by brushing your teeth several times a day to avoid suffering from tooth decay.

Using dental plaque as an example, I can easily illustrate the damage that biofilm does to mucous membranes. If you stand in front of the mirror and pull your lower lip forward, you can actually see the mucous membrane of your mouth quite clearly. In a healthy condition, the skin on the inside of the mouth, which is a beautiful pinkish red, shines from the layer of moisture on it. If you would stop brushing your teeth for a month or two, the biofilm in your mouth – the plaque – would rapidly multiply and spread across the surface. As a result, a white layer of deposits becomes visible throughout the mouth. It can even spread past the corners of the mouth to the outside.

Your mouth will start to feel very dry on the inside, and sores and cracks may appear in the skin. The mucous membrane no longer looks nice and pink and shiny. This is what happens when you don't adequately combat a very fast-growing biofilm, in this case, by brushing your teeth several times a day.

The situation in the gut is essentially exactly the same, except we can't brush it to remove the biofilm. We've already discussed the consequences of this. It directly and indirectly leads to all kinds of diseases. Fortunately, the solution is simple, something I explain further in Chapter 4.

## Irritated, infected, broken

An out-of-control biofilm that sticks to the intestinal wall eventually causes it to dry out, resulting in inflammation. If you were to study such an inflammation to see what was happening at the cellular level you would see the following: cells swelling to the point that the connecting links between them , the so-called tight junctions, snap off. It destroys the structure that connects the cells and marks the beginning of serious intestinal problems. Microscopic holes can form between the cells of your intestinal wall, which can allow all sorts of things to pass through that normally wouldn't, resulting in a condition called leaky gut syndrome.

If the intestinal wall is damaged, nutrients that have not yet been sufficiently digested can pass through the intestinal wall as oversized particles and be absorbed into the bloodstream. Fungi and viruses can also enter the blood through the microscopic holes. Your blood then reacts violently to these half-digested food particles, fungi and viruses, and sounds the alarm. Our body reacts by sending "soldiers" – white blood cells – to the half-digested food particles as these are seen as intruders. In this way, our immune system is activated to combat the half-digested food particles that have unintentionally entered the blood stream. This is the cause of all food hypersensitivities, allergies and autoimmune diseases.

This situation, unfortunately, is not exceptional. Most people in the Western world have an overgrowth of biofilm in their gut and, as a result, an inflamed intestinal wall to some degree. If that situation continues for too long, you become overweight, underweight, or you develop an illness or chronic symptoms. Even if you're living as healthily as you can, your body is probably still succumbing to the polluted environment.

### Antibiotics harm your gut

It's not just pollution that attacks the healthy bacteria in your gut. They can also be killed by antibiotics, which ruthlessly destroy all bacteria. Of course, with life-threatening pneumonia, you shouldn't refuse antibiotic treatment. With some ailments however, such as chronic acne, you'll be a lot better off with a change of diet, tea tree oil or silver ointment and some patience. The body has to work extremely hard after a course of antibiotics to regain proper acidity, which isn't easy in an environment where pollution is constantly assaulting the body.

Bad bacteria in your body also become a little more immune to antibiotics after each treatment, so it takes more effort each time to fight an infection. With antibiotics, you easily end up in a vicious cycle. People who suffer from frequent bladder infections and treat them with antibiotics can relate to this. In fact, inflammations in the urinary tract are caused by uncontrolled growth of the biofilm in that area. The biofilm contains harmful bacteria, but the antibiotics fight only the part of the harmful bacteria that are not enclosed in the biofilm. Harmful bacteria in biofilm are almost impossible to control with medication and are also becoming increasingly resistant to antibiotics. At the same time, antibiotics also fight the healthy bacteria, the bacteria your body actually does need. After a course of antibiotics the remaining healthy bacteria must produce new healthy gut flora from scratch, which is quite tricky in acidic environment.

Using antibiotics is like spraying a garden with an herbicide that not only kills the dandelions, but also your roses and your berry bushes, as well as polluting the soil to the point where new, desirable plants have little chance.

**Damaged gut flora due to antibiotics**
Kevin sought my advice after years of symptoms caused, in part, by antibiotics. The problems he faced started when he was young. He had terrible acne as adolescent. His dermatologist prescribed Clamoxyl, an antibiotic for skin infections. Major side effects include gastrointestinal symptoms. Kevin took it for two years and developed terrible bowel problems. He also developed anorexia and lived mostly on ice cream and licorice, completely wrecking his intestinal flora over the years.

During his search for a cure, Kevin became intrigued by naturopathic medicine. Mainstream medicine had nothing more to offer him, so what did he have to lose? He started eating more healthily. He added organic vegetables where possible, fruits, superfoods and various oils to his diet.

Despite his efforts to improve his health, his gut didn't improve. Kevin tried everything: homeopathy, bowel irrigation, probiotics, bioresonance and treatments with electromagnetic vibrations. Yet still he obtained no relief.

He eventually came to me and asked for advice then started the gut cure to discharge the biofilm. With additional supplements, his intestines recovered, though it took about a year and a half. Kevin is feeling much better now, and his mood has also improved tremendously.

## The biofilm contamination chart

If we express the contamination process and the formation of biofilm in your gut in a diagram, we see the following:

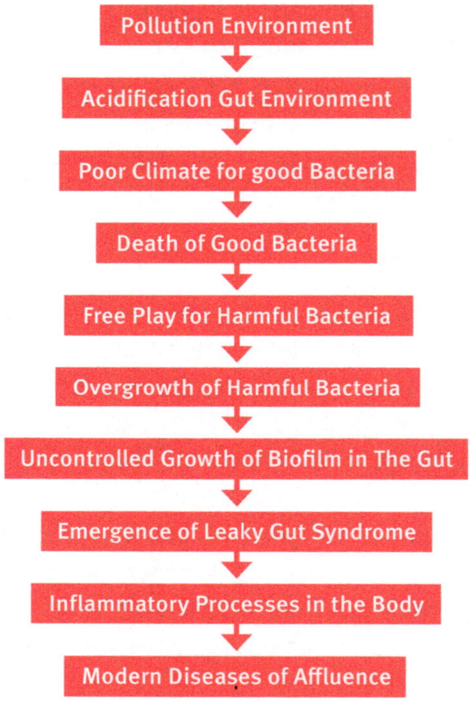


Figure 2.3 The process of uncontrolled biofilm formation

Figures 2.4 and 2.5 both show an intestinal wall. Figure 2.4 shows the intestinal wall with a healthy mucosa (thin and somewhat transparent) unthreatened by overgrown biofilm. In this situation, the healthy mucosa can protect the intestinal wall while keeping it permeable to nutrients, vitamins and minerals.

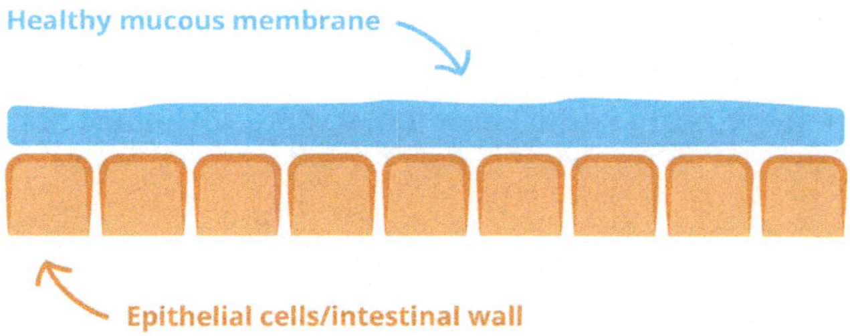


Figure 2.4 Healthy mucosa covers the intestinal wall.

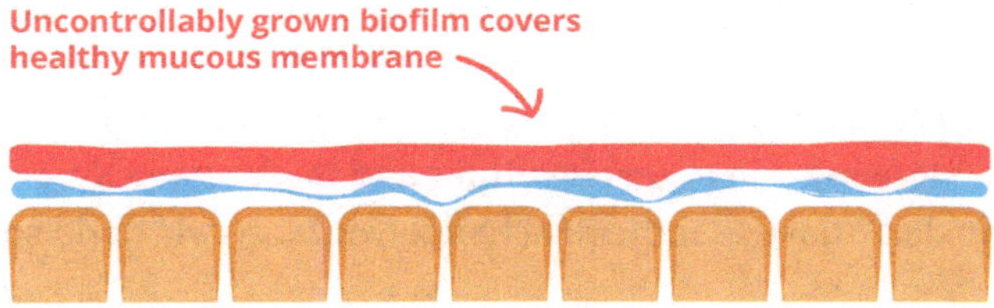


Figure 2.5 An biofilm growing uncontrollably sticks to the intestinal wall and irritates and infects the healthy mucosa.

Figure 2.5 shows the biofilm, in which pathogenic bacteria flourish and which also contains heavy metals, fungi and viruses. The biofilm sticks to the intestinal wall and dries out the healthy mucosa, affecting the intestinal wall's ability to properly absorb nutrients, vitamins and minerals in the process. In the end, this is what makes you ill.

## Knowledge about biofilm

The principle of biofilms is simple and logical and its existence has been established in several studies. Yet this knowledge is hardly widespread among specialists and is not taken into account in existing treatment methods. I'm sure you can imagine that when I first learned about biofilm, I was quite shocked. After all my training and practical experience I could rightfully call myself a gut expert, but nobody had ever taught me anything about the principle of biofilm. In fact, it was the missing link, the blind spot of educators and gut experts. I have made it my mission to spread this knowledge. At this point, you are in the know too, so take advantage of it.

## The good news and bad news

It will be clear to you by now that the biofilm growing in your gut can impact your health in various ways. A damaged gut wall can cause immune responses in the rest of your body which eventually become chronic: the so-called diseases of affluence. In the next chapter, you can read which chronic diseases originate in the gut. That may sound depressing, but the good news is that you can remove the biofilm, allowing you to feel healthier and more energetic. Better still, you don't have to radically change your lifestyle to do so.

## Summary

**The biofilm in your bowels: energy guzzler and pathogen**
Since the first half of the 20th century, our surroundings have become heavily polluted. Industrialization has brought artificial chemicals and heavy metals into our environment on a large scale, and through the air, water and soil, they have found their way into our foods and bodies. The exact effects of many chemicals on your body are still unknown. By the time this becomes clear, they'll have polluted our environment – and our bodies – for decades. Day after day, they pester the very organ that is meant to let nutrients through and block out toxins: your gut.

Our intestines are no match for this attack by pollution. As a result, biofilm can grow freely. The biofilm contains many harmful bacteria, heavy metals, viruses and fungi. It dries out the intestinal wall, infecting it and thus destroying it. It disrupts the absorption of good nutrients, vitamins and minerals by your intestines and fuels food hypersensitivities. This causes a lack of energy and makes you susceptible to disease. This is reflected, among other things, in the increase in chronic gastrointestinal and liver complaints and a growing number of people struggling with obesity. Fortunately, removing the biofilm is simple, offering you the chance to feel healthy and energetic again.

3

# We Have Become Ill and *Allergic* on a Mass Scale

*A frightening number of people suffer from modern diseases of affluence, such as allergies, cardiovascular disease, cancer, and numerous lung, brain and joint conditions. There is one common denominator here: they all start in your gut. The biofilm in the intestines causes leaky gut syndrome, and a leaky gut causes chronic inflammation throughout the body. These low-grade inflammations are the source of various diseases that, at first glance, have nothing to do with your gut, namely Alzheimer's, rheumatism and diabetes. Hence, a polluted gut not only causes food allergies and intestinal complaints, but chronic diseases of affluence as well. This chapter explains how.*

## Invisible inflammations

No matter where you live, the pollution in the air, food and water has a draining effect on your body. We all have biofilm in our gut, some more than others. All of us suffer from irritated or damaged intestines to a greater or lesser extent. The result is an excessively permeable intestinal wall which allows particles of food that have not yet been sufficiently digested to pass through the intestinal wall and enter the blood stream. This is a condition known as leaky gut syndrome. As long as the intestinal wall is still intact, only the most digested food particles can pass through, but with a leaky gut, particles that were not intended to be absorbed by the blood at all can suddenly pass through.

In response, your body sounds the alarm. Everything that enters the blood is analyzed by size and those undigested food particles now have the size of a virus or bacteria, so the body starts attacking them. As a result, the immune system springs into action and a substance is formed that triggers an inflammatory response.

Most people notice little to nothing of this, but the tricky thing is that it's a never-ending process that can have major long-term consequences. It causes weak inflammatory responses – "low-grade inflammations" – in various parts of your body. You don't register them because they are not associated with fever or pain, but they're there all the same.

If those inflammations simmer long enough, issues can arise in many areas of your body, eventually culminating in diseases of affluence. These diseases were once very rare and have emerged as a result of our modern lifestyle, where we ingest many unhealthy substances. Combined with prolonged stress and the fast pace of Western life, this is making us ill on a massive scale. These illnesses may seem to come out of nowhere, but they are actually result of long term, low grade inflammation, brought on by exposure to pollution.
This is not just a theory, numerous studies have demonstrated the mechanism. I will highlight a groundbreaking, large scale study, which revealed that this 'cold' inflammation is the cause of many diseases of affluence.

**USA study: many diseases of affluence start in the gut**

A clinical trial conducted in 2017 by two cardiologists from Brigham and Women's Hospital in Boston has indicated that common chronic diseases – Alzheimer's, asthma, osteoarthritis, psoriasis, anemia, Parkinson's, multiple sclerosis, diabetes, depression – are triggered by low-grade inflammation, which originates in the gut. The study, which was conducted among 10,000 patients in 39 countries, was designed to measure the effects of using anti-inflammatory drugs in patients with cardiovascular disease and other diseases of affluence, such as cancer and rheumatoid arthritis.

The result? Mortality rates and the number of reported symptoms plummeted. In lung cancer, the mortality rate dropped by as much as 77 percent. Reports of rheumatic arthritis also decreased significantly. To the researchers, this was proof that chronic immune responses, which trigger inflammation, are the source of many more diseases than we previously thought.

This low grade inflammation is caused by the immune response of the blood in leaky gut syndrome, thus allowing us to conclude that many diseases of affluence originate in the gut.

*Source: Shaw, 2019*

## From biofilm to inflammation

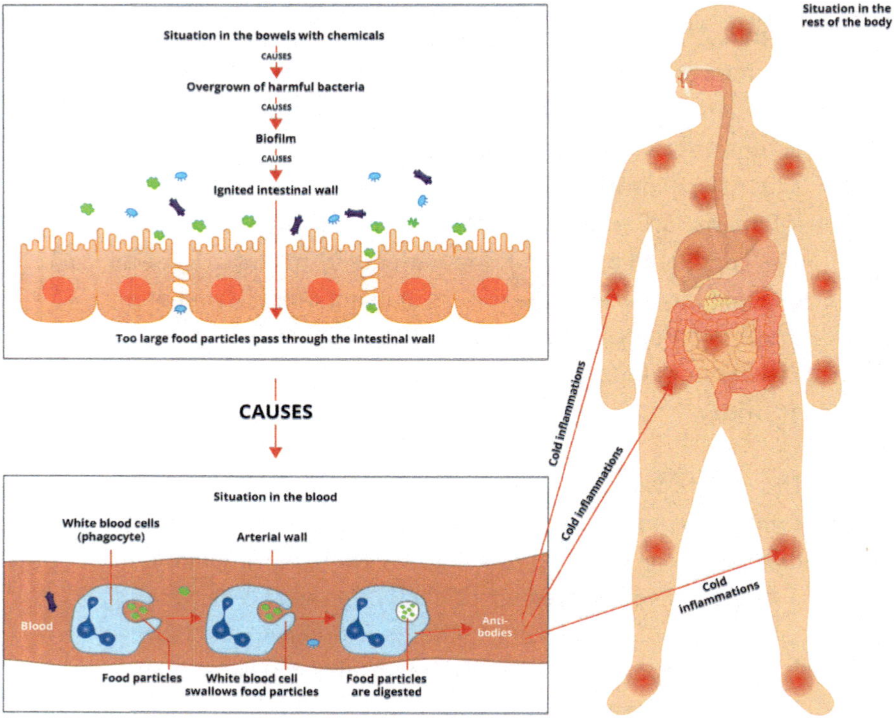


Figure 3.1 Pollution in your gut eventually leads to low-grade inflammation in your body.

## Invisible immune response

With a severe immune response to, say, a viral or bacterial infection, you feel sick and develop a fever, which is easy to measure. Low-grade inflammation caused by leaky gut syndrome, however, almost always goes unnoticed. Within mainstream health care, nothing can be detected at this stage because there's no tissue damage, at least not yet.

Laboratory tests exist to detect this type of inflammation, but they are sparse, not widely used (these are not the common allergy or immune tests) and very expensive. So, it's quite possible to demonstrate low grade inflammation medically, but it's far from common practice.

That invisibility of the immune response is also part of the problem. Your body is highly effective at accomplishing its most important tasks, so the threat must be extremely serious for the alarm bells to go off in the form of fever and illness. Furthermore, a triggered immune response is only effective – and harmless – for a brief period of time. With an overly permeable gut however, immune responses are generated continuously, day after day, year after year. This is extremely exhausting for your body and your immune system has to work overtime.

In some people this causes the immune system to go into overdrive. Your defenses will not only attack those oversized, leaked through food particles, but also your own bodily tissues. This is how notorious autoimmune responses, such as ulcerative colitis, type 1 diabetes and MS, arise, attacking healthy cells and damaging your organs.

## From low grade inflammation to diseases of affluence

It will be clear to you by now that the biofilm in your gut can eventually cause a lot of damage in your body, this is the onset of illness. I am definitely not saying this to worry you, the fact of having a biofilm in your gut doesn't mean that you will necessarily get sick. There are people who never develop any complaints. My main purposer is to make you aware of what is going on in your body, then when symptoms do arise, you can look beyond the symptoms alone. Understanding the process gives you the knowledge to address those complaints at their source: the biofilm. Even better, this is less complicated than you might think. More about this in chapter 4.

What diseases can be caused by an overly permeable gut? The most prevalent illnesses are described below. Whether a person develops an illness and which one, depends on a variety of factors. It would be going too far to explain that mechanism here. One thing I can say: the weakest link breaks the chain. In other words, the area in your body which is the least strong is the most susceptible to developing disease. Want to know more about these diseases and how they arise? In the bibliography of this book, I refer to articles, scientific and otherwise which explain what is going on in more detail.

### *Intestinal diseases*

*Ulcerative colitis, Crohn's disease, colorectal cancer and irritable bowel syndrome (IBS)*

Intestinal diseases are widespread. As already stated above, in the US about 60 to 70 million people are affected by one of the many digestive diseases, roughly 18 percent of the population.

These intestinal diseases are considered "chronic", meaning that mainstream medical science has no solution for them. Treatment often consists of anti-inflammatories, combined with a lifelong diet and lifestyle adjustments.

The cause of these intestinal problems is easy to pinpoint: the biofilm that damages the intestinal wall and results in inflammation and a leaky gut, leading to a whole range of intestinal diseases. The body's immune response causes the gut to become even more inflamed in many places, resulting in conditions such as colitis ulcerosa, Crohn's disease, colorectal cancer and IBS.

**Extra energy through intestinal cleansing**
Theo, a 45-year-old construction worker, came to me several years ago with severe pain in the stomach and around the gallbladder. He had suffered from this since adolescence, and it constrained him in his work. He had consulted a regular doctor, who wasn't able to find the cause for his pain.

During the anamnesis, in which I discuss the client's medical history and symptoms, he told me he had suffered from meningitis as a young child after drinking ditch water. At the time, Theo lived in an agricultural area where farmers used to spray DDT to control weeds. DDT washes away into the surrounding ditch and groundwater, so it could easily have been in the ditch water that Theo ingested.

Theo's meningitis was treated with a high dose of antibiotics. I concluded that both the DDT and the antibiotics had contaminated and disrupted his intestines, which explained his pain. After a thorough cleansing of his gut and the rest of his body, Theo made an excellent recovery. His renewed energy enabled him to be able to work comfortably again.

### *Alzheimer's and other types of dementia*
Alzheimer's, a form of dementia which is caused by a malfunctioning in the brain is unfortunately not an uncommon disease. Currently, more than 55 million people worldwide suffer from dementia and every year there are nearly 10 million new cases. Medical science still has no solution for this chronic disease, which damages more and more parts of the brain, until death follows. There is medication available that attempts to influence symptoms and reduce memory loss.

The deterioration of the brain is caused by a buildup of the harmful protein amyloid, which results in the formation of "plaques" or deposits. As a result of these plaques, the communication between brain cells is obstructed.

You may wonder about the connection between Alzheimer's and a contaminated gut. Well, bad gut bacteria can produce amyloid. A leaky gut allows the harmful protein to enter the bloodstream and, by destroying the cell membrane of nerve cells, it can gain access to the brain, where it can form plaques between nerve cells. To make matters worse, part of the broken cell membrane can enter the bloodstream and trigger a chronic inflammatory process there that contributes to the damage and deterioration of the brain.

### *Osteoarthritis and other forms of rheumatic disorders*

Rheumatism is a collective term for the more than one hundred different disorders of the joints, muscles and tendons. Worldwide, rheumatoid arthritis affects about 1 percent of the population and about 0.6 percent of the US population. The annual incidence of rheumatoid arthritis has been estimated to be about 4 per 100,000. That means, each year, 40 new cases of RA will be diagnosed for every 100,000 people.

In rheumatic disorders, the body's immune system becomes dysregulated, causing chronic inflammation. In osteoarthritis, which is a form of rheumatoid arthritis, the cartilage in the joints becomes thinner, softer and is prone to crumble. This can lead to bone deformation directly beneath the cartilage. Visible and palpable nodules form at the edge of the joint that restrict the joint's range of motion. Osteoarthritis is most common in knees, hips, fingers, thumbs, big toes, the neck and lower back. Mainstream medical science has no solution for osteoarthritis. Medicinal injections, however, can sometimes help patients move better.

The cause for osteoarthritis and other rheumatic disorders can also be found in leaky gut syndrome. The immune response triggered by the leaky gut can involve the production of a substance called TNF-alpha which causes rheumatoid arthritis. This triggers rheumatic inflammation in the joints, damaging them in the process.

**Less rheumatism due to intestinal detoxification**
Maria, a retired secretary, had greatly looked forward to retirement. She and her partner lived by the water, and they had a boat they loved to go out on. Unfortunately, she had severe rheumatism in her arms and hands. Everything hurt, not just the untying of the mooring lines, but also the simple act of picking up her cup of coffee as she sat on deck.

Rheumatism is caused by inflammation, which is caused by an overly polluted and permeable gut. So I started with detoxification, a colon cleansing regimen and additional preparations to eliminate the heavy metals from her body. Measurements with an electronic acupuncture machine indicated that her body contained too many heavy metals. I also discovered that she had a relatively unknown metabolic disorder: hemopyrrollactamuria (HPU) which robs the body of important minerals and vitamins, including B6, zinc and manganese. To resolve this, I prescribed additional vitamins for her to take. This restored her energy.

She also suffered from tooth infections, which exacerbated inflammation in the rest of the body. A biological dentist was able to solve that.

After this substantial course of treatment, not only did she have far fewer symptoms, but she also lost a whopping

33 pounds. She looked great and years younger. To her astonishment she even received some envious responses from those around her. She took great pleasure in her newly acquired health.

### *Asthma and COPD*

In Asthma, the lungs don't function properly due to inflammation of the mucous membrane in the alveoli, causing the lung tubes to narrow. Asthma is a chronic condition. Small inflammations are always present in the lungs. With COPD (chronic obstructive pulmonary disease), you suffer from chronic narrowing of the lung tubes because the alveoli have become inflamed and damaged.

In the US, approximately 25 million people have asthma, about 1 in 13 people. This number is expected to continue to rise in the coming years. Mainstream medical science cannot cure asthma and COPD. Many patients do have an inhaler that allows them to inhale anti-inflammatories and airway dilating medication when they experience symptoms. Lifestyle adjustments, such as quitting smoking, can reduce symptoms and make COPD less likely to worsen.

Both asthma and COPD are originally inflammatory diseases. Again, a clear link can be made to a polluted and therefore overly permeable gut, causing small chronic inflammatory reactions throughout the body.

### *Anemia*

Anemia occurs when there is too little hemoglobin in your blood. The protein hemoglobin (Hb) transports oxygen from your lungs to your organs. If that transport is not optimum, you may experience fatigue, shortness of breath, dizziness, a feeling that you might faint, heart palpitations, sweating, headaches and tinnitus. Severe anemia

may involve pallor as well as abdominal pain and diarrhea. Anemia symptoms cause you to feel unwell on a regular basis and prevent you from functioning optimally in your daily work and life. People suffering from anemia are usually prescribed iron supplements, (iron is the oxygen-binding component in hemoglobin).
Research has shown that the most common form of anemia begins with chronic inflammation in the gut, due to pollution and an overgrowth of harmful bacteria. The resulting biofilm obstructs the small intestine from absorbing enough iron.

A deficiency of vitamin B12 and folic acid can also be the cause of anemia, as it prevents the body from making enough red blood cells. Red blood cells contain high amounts of hemoglobin, so if fewer are available, less oxygen can be transported through the body. Harmful bacteria in the gut absorb the B12, so a deficiency easily occurs.

### *Depression*
Depression is a mental illness which is associated with a lack of certain neurotransmitters in the brain. According to CDC reports, 4.7 percent of US adults aged 18 and over, experience regular feelings of depression. About half of the people who suffer from depression recover within three months. For others, the depression returns after a period of recovery.

As you've read in Chapter 1, most neurotransmitters are formed in the gut. If production falters in the gut, which happens when it becomes too polluted, this is a serious matter because the brain can only function properly with sufficient neurotransmitters. Vitamin B12 or magnesium deficiencies complicate the production of neurotransmitters in the gut and thus lead to a higher risk of depression. These deficiencies occur when the good gut bacteria are not functioning properly (due to excessive pollution) or because you're not ingesting enough of them in your current diet.

In addition, a leaky gut can cause chronic inflammatory responses in the brain via immune responses in the blood. The brain responds by producing stress hormones, which can lead to feelings of depression as well, thus trapping you in a vicious circle.

**Depressed by the sweetener**
Joshua, a 52-year-old flower shop owner, came to me feeling severely depressed. He didn't see the point in life anymore. His symptoms were so severe that I suspected a serious physical cause for his problem. I decided to measure him immediately with my electroacupuncture device, which assesses the functioning of all organs and organ systems. If one or more organs are not functioning at their optimum, I can determine what's causing it. To my great surprise, I found a very high concentration of toxins in his nervous system. After asking a lot of questions, the cause turned out to be artificial sweeteners. When I asked him if he used sweeteners and if so, how many, his answer was, "Yes, but not that many. Just two in my coffee." But when I asked him how much coffee he drank in a day, this turned out to be as many as 15 cups. Thirty sweeteners a day.

I gave him a detox treatment to cleanse his bowels, and the advice to drink only two cups of coffee a day and use stevia instead of sweetener. Stevia is a plant-based sweetener, while aspartame is a chemical one.

During his next appointment a week later, in which I wanted to offer him mental therapy, he told me he had actually wanted to cancel our appointment. He felt so good, he told me: "I haven't felt depressed for a moment since."

## *Diabetes*

Diabetes is a chronic metabolic disease characterized by excessive levels of glucose (sugar) in the blood. Glucose is derived from the carbohydrates in your diet and is transported through the blood to all the body's cells. The cells use it as fuel, allowing us to move, grow and live. Insulin, which is produced in the pancreas, is needed to transmit glucose into the cells. When the pancreas doesn't produce enough insulin, this creates a shortage of glucose for the cells. Due to that deficiency, the glucose levels in the blood remain too high while the glucose levels in the cells are too low, preventing them from performing their tasks.

As per reports of the CDC:
37.3 million people have diabetes. That is 11.3 percent of the US population.
28.7 million people have been diagnosed with diabetes.
8.5 million people who have diabetes have not been diagnosed and do not know they have it.
96 million adults have prediabetes.

In type 2 diabetes, the pancreas does make insulin, but low-grade inflammations prevent the insulin from entering cells through the blood. The blood sugar level (glucose level) becomes too high, while the cells run out. Type 1 diabetes has a different cause. With type 1, the pancreas no longer produces any insulin, which is unrelated to low-grade inflammations.

**Use insulin or eat healthier?**

Accountant Frank (59) was considerably overweight when he visited my practice for the first time. He had been diagnosed with type 2 diabetes, a form of diabetes that is usually caused by an unhealthy lifestyle and leaky gut syndrome. For many years, he had been using insulin to get his blood glucose levels down. As this form of diabetes is associated with a leaky gut, I prescribed a 12-day colon cleanse and explained how a healthier diet would help him. This included no more coffee, no gluten, dairy, sugar or artificial sweeteners. He instantly lost many pounds. The best part, however, was that his blood sugar remained stable after the colon cleanse, so he no longer had to inject insulin. Unfortunately, after the cure, he fell back into his old habits, eating lots of fat and sugar and very few vegetables. So gradually, he had to go back on insulin.

**Avoid artificial sweeteners and coffee**

Diabetics like Frank often think that traditional sugars and carbohydrates, found in pasta, potatoes and candy, are the only threats to healthy sugar levels. Research indicates, however, that artificial sweeteners, such as aspartame (E951), sucralose (E955) and saccharin (E954), also disrupt a diabetic's blood sugar levels.

According to another study, coffee is not harmless either. In fact, caffeine can reduce the cells' sensitivity to insulin. It raises blood sugar levels. The body responds by making more insulin causing the insulin levels in the blood rise. So, for diabetics – who already have high insulin levels in their blood – coffee makes matters worse. It becomes increasingly difficult for glucose to enter the cells in order to be converted into energy.

### *Cancer*

In cancer, the hereditary material of a cell changes. It then no longer follows the normal cycle of dividing, growing and dying, but proliferates and forms a tumor. In cell proliferation, the cell loses its original function. Cancer often originates in one organ, but can spread – metastasize – through the body via the blood or lymph nodes. There are over a hundred different types of cancer. According to CDC reports, in the United States in 2019, 1,752,735 new cancer cases were reported and 599,589 people died of cancer. For every 100,000 people, 439 new cancer cases were reported with 146 people dying of cancer each year. Regular health care treats patients with a combination of surgery, radiation, chemotherapy and hormone therapy. In recent years, immunotherapy, in which cancer patients' immune cells are "trained" to resist the cell proliferations in their bodies, has become increasingly common.

Research has demonstrated the link between a leaky gut and cancer. When the gut allows oversized food particles to pass through, this causes low grade inflammations. These can affect the DNA in the cells, causing the cells to fester. This proliferation is further boosted by a polluted gut. When the body is unable to get rid of the abundance of chemicals and heavy metals, they are stored in the tissues. This accumulation of toxins makes the cells more susceptible to proliferation.

### *Multiple sclerosis*

Multiple sclerosis (MS) is a chronic disease of the central nervous system, which consists of a network of billions of nerve cells or neurons. They are coated with a protective protein called myelin that serves as insulation. When that myelin is affected – by hardening (sclerosing) in the form of so-called "plaques" – signals can no longer be sent properly from A to B and your central nervous system can no longer control your body properly. The hardening of nerve cells can be seen on an MRI scan as plaques.

Recent findings from the National MS Society estimate that nearly 1 million people in the United States are living with the disease, about one in a thousand. This is more than double the last reported number and the first national research on MS prevalence since 1975. An estimated 2.5 million people live with MS worldwide. An estimated 200 new cases are diagnosed each week in the United States, according to the MS Discovery Forum. Doctors typically try to contain symptoms with muscle relaxants, painkillers and anti-inflammatories that suppress immune responses, reducing the risk of infection.

A leaky gut, as you now know, can cause inflammation anywhere in the body and trigger an immune response. The antibodies formed can affect the protective myelin around your nerves which results in nerve impairment. Therefore, as research has indicated, curing a leaky gut may potentially relieve MS symptoms.

### *Parkinson's disease*

Parkinson's disease is a progressive brain disorder that affects the control of muscle movements. Parkinson's often involves trembling (when a person tries to stand or sit still) and slower movement, typically concentrated on one side of the body. Fine motor skills can be a problem as well. Fatigue, "freezing" (unable to walk any further), a mask-like facial expression (stiffened face), softer speech, difficulty swallowing, drooling, impaired sense of smell, difficulty urinating, sleep disturbances and sexual problems are also common symptoms. Parkinson's patients are more likely to have dementia, depression and bowel obstruction. The number of symptoms and the degree to which these occur, plus the fact that they continue to get worse, make Parkinson's a highly strenuous disease.

Parkinson's disease is generally not curable. Therefore, treatment is primarily focused on retaining as much function as possible with the help of physical therapy and speech therapy, for example. Medication can also supplement dopamine deficiency and reduce stiffness and sluggishness. In advanced stages, medication through a pump or brain surgery may be required.

In scientific research, the development of Parkinson's is commonly associated with heavy metals and chemicals accumulating in the body. Such pollution contributes to the growth of bad bacteria, which cause biofilm overgrowth. That biofilm, in turn, can cause a leaking gut. We can conclude, therefore, that pollution is an important explanation for the development of Parkinson's disease.

### *Psoriasis*

Psoriasis is a skin condition that causes a rash with itchy, scaly patches. In patients with psoriasis, the production of new skin cells is accelerated, and excess skin layers are not shed. This creates an accumulation of several skin layers consisting of immature skin cells that are difficult to peel off. The white scaly patches are often found on the elbows, the lower back and scalp. If they are removed, bleeding may occur.

According to the National Psoriasis Foundation, more than 8 million people in the United States have psoriasis. About 2-3 percent of the world's population has it, 125 million people. The symptoms of this common skin condition are treated with skin ointments, light therapy, and medication to combat skin peeling, inhibit inflammation or suppress the immune system.

The cause for this condition can be found in the gut as well. A leaky gut causes an immune response in the blood, which can turn against its own skin. This is what happens in psoriasis. The accumulated antibodies cause skin cells to renew too quickly and cause an inflammatory reaction in the skin. As a result, blood vessels dilate, transporting more blood and a variety of anti-inflammatory substances to the skin. Psoriasis is almost always accompanied by a leaky gut and, as research shows, can also be treated by addressing it.

**Psoriasis nearly gone through colon cleansing and diet**
Diana, a lovely 35-year-old woman, suffered from skin inflammation, accompanied by severe itchiness. Psoriasis, was her dermatologist's diagnosis. Psoriasis is not just unsightly, Diana realized, her skin symptoms meant something was wrong in her body. That's why she came to me.

Looking at her symptoms, I instantly knew I was dealing with a leaky gut. I asked her to do a blood test to find out which nutrients were traveling through her intestinal wall as oversized, undigested particles and causing the inflammation that had become visible through her skin. This resulted in a list of foods she should not consume for an initial two months. I then proceeded to cleanse her bowels, which were bound to be severely contaminated due to the leaky gut. After the cleanse, I gave her a remedy to repair the intestinal wall, allowing the leaky gut to heal.

The result? The spots on her skin disappeared. However, she did have to remain careful with certain foods. Nevertheless, she ended up feeling much better and even became pregnant, something she had tried but failed to do for years.

### *Allergies, food intolerances and food sensitivities*

According to statistics issued by the CDC, 31.8 percent of the people in the US aged over 18 suffer from allergies of all kinds. This is compared to 27.2 percent of people under the age of 18.

One can be sensitive or intolerant to any type of food. The most common allergic reactions diagnosable to doctors are caused by the proteins in cow's milk, chicken eggs, peanuts, nuts, seafood, apple, peach, soy and gluten. If you're allergic to something, you'll have a reaction within minutes to a few hours of eating it. This can be a mild response, causing weariness for example, or a very severe one like osteoporosis. A peanut allergy can even kill you.

In addition to the medically recognized allergies, there are certain food intolerances that practically everyone suffers from without knowing it. These intolerances and sensitivities to foods are not easily diagnosed, but they do cause issues. You can be sensitive to many different foods, from carrots to parsley. If you're allergic or sensitive to something you eat, you can of course make sure that you simply don't eat it. It gets tricky though, when a particular substance is found in a lot of foods, such as lactose (milk protein allergy) or gluten (celiac disease). With a lactose or gluten allergy, you become quite limited in what you can eat.

The fact that you have a food allergy or intolerance doesn't mean these foods – gluten and lactose, for example – are necessarily bad for your body. The allergic reaction you're suffering from is caused by a leaky gut, often combined with a lack of the enzymes you need to digest milk (lactose enzyme) or wheat bread (carbohydrate enzyme). If the gut is too permeable, the blood sounds a huge alarm when lactose and gluten are detected and starts producing antibodies, such as histamine. Each time the body recognizes such a food particle, it goes into overdrive. As a result, an immune response is triggered, which creates the allergic reaction.

## How can you heal your gut?

The reason I describe all these illnesses in this chapter is because I want to give you a sense of the gravity of the situation. I want to create awareness that the biofilm in your gut can do a lot of damage sooner or later and may have already done so. However, I won't stop there. My most important message is that you can do something to change the situation for the better. Your body is infinitely powerful at repairing itself, especially if you give it a little push in the right direction.

There are numerous ways to cleanse your gut, I have tried many of them myself. A highly effective colon cleansing method exists that can rid you of your biofilm. In the following chapters, I'll explain how it works and how to heal your damaged gut afterwards.

## Summary

**The major effects of biofilm in your gut**

The number of people suffering from modern diseases of affluence is huge and the impact on a person's life and those closest to them is significant. The list of diseases includes such things as dementia, lung conditions, rheumatoid arthritis, depression, diabetes, cancer, MS, Parkinson's disease, allergies, intolerances and skin conditions. These conditions, as the name suggests, are linked to our high levels of affluence. They are caused in part by chronic low grade inflammation. These "cold" inflammations are caused by the biofilm in your gut, which can grow due to the pollution you are constantly exposed to as a result of our high level of affluence.

Low-grade inflammation in itself is not directly harmful, it's actually an effective clearance method of your immune system to fight off unwanted invaders in your blood. However, once you live with that biofilm in your gut and a permeable intestinal wall for a long time, the immune response becomes chronic and it becomes a ticking time bomb. Whether it goes off and where it goes off, depends on many factors. Not everyone with a leaky gut gets sick or develops symptoms, but it is important to be aware of the underlying cause of many complaints and especially of what you can do about them.

4

# Healthy and Energetic with a *Clean* Gut

*We all want to look and feel good. We'd like to grow old, without feeling old. Not surprisingly, a huge industry has emerged built around staying youthful and aging with vitality. Countless remedies exist for this purpose, but how effective are they really? There are also many different gut cleansing options available. As a naturopath, I have explored, researched and tested many of them. So far I have found only one way to safely and gently rid you of the biofilm in your gut. You'll read more about it in this chapter. The reason I'm so excited about this is because it can help you stay healthy, energetic and slim for as long as possible – with very few restrictions.*

## My quest for health and how it all started

I was 18 years old when I started studying naturopathy. I followed classes among doctors and therapists who were all at least 20 years my senior. The program offered in-depth and thorough knowledge of everything related to colon cleansing. In natural medicine, "detoxification" was key. By making sure the body got rid of all toxins, energy was released and the body could begin to heal itself. Fewer toxins in the brain would allow you to start thinking more clearly. A body that's in top condition would also be much less prone to aging. The inevitable deterioration could be halted by gut detoxification. Back then we had enemas, juice cures, supplements and herbal mixtures at our disposal for this purpose.

These approaches are still relevant, although new and more effective methods have since become available. After my education, I worked as a sales representative for a manufacturer of natural medicine. I visited countless therapists and doctors and soon I knew better than anyone what products were available in the field of colon cleansing remedies and cures. I knew what worked, what didn't work and why. From my previously acquired broad theoretical knowledge and the experiences of other experts in practice, I devised a program using the resources available at the time, which I applied when I opened my own practice.

## Fitter and healthier

I offered six week cures, consisting of strict diet and colon irrigation twice a week. I had devised it in such a way that it was easy to sustain despite the restrictions. People could eat as much as they desired, but only fresh, natural produce, cooked or as a salad. Everyone who visited my practice became fitter, healthier and more energetic due to the treatments. People with chronic illnesses and obesity achieved fantastic results with an additional twice-a-year juice cleanse. Intense symptoms, from intestinal illnesses to rheumatic disorders, diabetes and eczema, faded or almost disappeared completely. It was, however, a tough cure for my clients and the colon irrigation was not always easy.

In those early days, I worked with whatever options were available, and they weren't exactly high tech. When the first fully automatic bowel cleanser came on the market, I immediately purchased one. This was the colon hydrotherapy machine ("hydro" from water). I also had an electroacupuncture device that allowed me to measure the energy of all internal organs. With this device, you can determine by objective measurement whether an organ is still functioning properly long before problems with such an organ occur. It turned out to be an important tool to gain insight into the effects of my treatments. I noticed that the cures were, for the most part, having the intended effect. One area proved to be beyond reach: the small intestine. Technically, it simply wasn't possible to flush this part of the body.

## The next phase

My mission was clear. I had to find a way to cleanse the small intestine. This became the next stage in my quest. I started by gathering all the internal bowel cleansing cures available at the time and subjecting them to close scrutiny. I used the best of them with clients for whom the usual treatments showed insufficient results. Unfortunately, none of these remedies proved to be sufficiently effective. The measurements did show some improvement, but not enough and not in all areas. On top of that, unpleasant side effects often occurred.

The downside of common remedies to cleanse the small intestine is that they're based on abrasives or enzymes. These abrasives, such as clay particles or psyllium fibers, have the side effect of irritating the intestinal wall. Since the intestinal wall would *already* be irritated and inflamed to a greater or lesser extent from pollution and the biofilm, I found these treatments less than ideal.

Enzyme based products work in a different way, they essentially dissolve the biofilm in the gut. This means that they do address the problem, but in the process create a bunch of new problems. Once you start breaking open the biofilm with enzymes, all the harmful bacteria trapped inside are released at once, and they enter the blood stream. It works, but clients could get quite sick from it. In other words, this cure could be worse than the disease. Based on these findings, such methods didn't qualify for use in my practice.

## An astounding result

By now I realized that despite all the remedies I used in my practice to help my clients, the biofilm remained. No amount of flushing agent or herbal mixture, no matter how aggressive, could remove the biofilm. I was fumbling around in the dark. I visited conferences and institutes all over the world and whenever possible, I also underwent all treatments and cures myself.

Then one day I received a tip from an American colleague, who told me that there was a remedy that could cleanse the entire intestinal system without any of the aforementioned side effects. I managed to get hold of this product with great difficulty and tested it on myself first. I had already seen pictures on the internet of users showing huge pieces of biofilm that had come out as a result.

Since I had been doing one or two colon flushes and fasting cures every year and by now had tried almost every colon cleansing product available, I didn't expect this remedy to have much effect on me. Which is why I was absolutely stunned when I witnessed what came out of me after the very first day (see picture).

This is the original photo demonstrating the effect this remedy had on me. Nothing has been photoshopped or altered, you can see my hand in a yellow housekeeping glove above our wood-colored toilet seat. For nearly three days following that morning, I was utterly perplexed. I simply couldn't believe this was possible, especially after a lifetime of yearly fasting cures, regular colon irrigation and all the other colon cleansing products I had tested. I couldn't wrap my head around it.

## The proof

I had now actually seen the biofilm, but more importantly, I felt the effect it had on me now that I'd lost it. I didn't need the electroacupuncture device to show me the impact of this remedy, but measured myself anyway. The outcome confirmed what I already knew: the cure worked. This profound experience made me determined to find out everything there was to know about this method.

After I did the cure, I contacted the manufacturer of the product to find out exactly how it worked. The manufacturer taught me all about the true nature of intestinal pollution. To my great surprise, the keyword here was something I'd never heard of before: biofilm.

I was excited and shocked at the same time. In all the years that I had studied the gut, during my education, at training sessions, no one ever mentioned the biofilm. However, this turned out to be the missing link, the source of everything.

For the first time, here was a product that didn't destroy the biofilm during the cleanse, but merely moistened it and caused it to swell, allowing it to leave the body without disintegrating. That was an important condition because if you force your body to excrete all that doesn't belong in the gut, for example with those enzyme-based agents, a piece of the biofilm dissolves and many harmful bacteria are released. Those bacteria can enter the blood through the intestinal wall. Then your poor body has to clean it all up.

During my training at the Academie voor Natuurgeneeskunde (Academy of Naturopathy), which was considered to be one of the best programs on the subject at the time, no one had ever so much as mentioned the phenomenon of "biofilm". Nor was it included in any of the other courses I took afterwards or addressed by one of the many experts I spoke to, whether this was about bowel cleansing or about health in general.

All the while, biofilm is the biggest source of trouble in our gut. It's not just in our bowels, our body is filled with all types of biofilm anywhere there is moisture. This is a scientific fact. Yet you hardly ever hear anything about it, even in medical reports.

Once I knew about the existence of biofilm, I delved into the matter and underwent thorough training with a German specialist in the field. Very little knowledge existed within my industry or in mainstream health care regarding biofilm formation in the gut – and very little is known of its enormous impact to this day.

## Biofilm in nature

Where there is moisture, there is biofilm. Many types of biofilm can be observed in the world around us. Biofilm forms when bacteria adhere to pipes and around drains, coating the inside of sewer pipes with a thick layer. The slimy layer you'll find in a vase of flowers if you leave them out for too long is also biofilm, as is the goo you can find in a ditch or the white deposit on the bottom of your dishwasher's filter. At water treatment plants, biofilm is enemy No. 1 of pipes, which are always in danger of silting up as a result. Swimming pool installations and pond pumps also struggle with it. The presence of biofilm is a fact of life, we cannot escape it. It's in our bodies as well.

The biofilm in our bodies can be found in many forms and various places. Those who deal with it professionally, such as general practitioners and medical specialists, are familiar with it. Yet the prevalence of biofilm in the gut is disputed by some experts, as if the same biological processes would not occur there. There is biofilm in our sinuses, ureters, vagina, bladder, eyes, wounds and – most commonly known in the form of plaque – the mouth. Now, as scientific research has revealed, we know you can also find it in the gut.

## Survival

Everyone has biofilm in their gut, some more than others. It has always been there, but people were less bothered by it in the past. The difference between then and now is that environmental pollution leads to an overgrowth of bad bacteria which then form more biofilm than before. It is much more than nature ever intended. These days, the water, air and soil in which our food grows – and the food itself – are no longer pure. The implications for our gut are huge.

All types of pathogenic bacteria protect themselves with a tough mucus layer. They cluster together and form the biofilm. They thrive in the polluted gut and start to multiply. This is a natural biological process. Everything in nature is focused on survival. This type of bacteria simply survives best in large numbers, close together, in an acidified environment full of harmful substances.

Good bacteria merely have a thin mucus layer, making them highly vulnerable. In a severely acidified environment, they become smothered and perish, further upsetting the balance between good and bad bacteria. To break out of this situation, it is important to be relieved of the biofilm in the gut.

## The ideal remedy

I was extremely happy to have found a remedy that could easily remove the biofilm, one which didn't damage the intestinal wall. The remedy, which contains a special fiber and okra plant powder, penetrates the biofilm without attacking or destroying it. The okra powder can absorb more than a hundred times its own weight in water. This "inflates" and moisturizes the biofilm so that it detaches from the intestinal wall and comes sliding to the exit along with the remedy. It causes little to no cramps or unpleasantness in the abdomen and certainly no diarrhea.

My search for the perfect solution to cleanse the *entire* intestinal system had come to an end. Finally, I could prescribe a safe, easy and effective cure in my practice. As I expected, the measurements of both the large and small intestines of my clients after using the new remedy greatly improved.
With this book, I hope to reach more people who have been struggling with their health for years. But most of all, I sincerely hope it will be read by those who have not yet developed any complaints. Because everyone who lives in the Western world today

has a layer of biofilm stuck to their gut wall. That includes you, dear reader, and sooner or later it will affect your health.

## Older and wiser?

From pre-historic times, we were designed as creatures that roam the savannah. Our bodies are equipped for lots of exercise, unprocessed foods and a clean environment. Even with a super healthy lifestyle, you're never going to reach that level these days. On the other hand, there is no need for nostalgia. Back then, human beings usually didn't live beyond thirty or forty. This does address the core issue though. How is it that, despite all our clever inventions and highly developed medical knowledge, we're not any healthier, even though we're living so much longer? Even if you don't get sick, getting older is quite a challenge. And the crazy thing is that we accept it. We think it's normal. "Age takes its toll," we say.

Here's what we think we know. As you get older, your body doesn't heal as easily. You're more susceptible to disease. You become stiffer. All your senses deteriorate little by little. Your metabolism slows down. Losing weight becomes more difficult, and staying active less successful. All these symptoms, however, are not caused by aging itself. It's the result of the accumulation of years of exposure to harmful substances. Your metabolism is not functioning as it should because your gut can't do its job properly. You're more susceptible to illness and ailments because there aren't enough good bacteria in your gut to uphold your resistance.

## Prevention is the best cure

Early aging is just one of the many consequences of the biofilm in your gut. It's an issue we all face. It could even be much worse. I discussed all the diseases, allergies and complications caused by a leaky gut in detail in the previous chapter.

I was, and still am, incredibly happy that there is now a program that shows wonderful results, even in the more severe cases. That said, with this accessible colon cure I especially hope to reach those people who are at an earlier stage. Prevention is the best cure. People who claim to be healthy are often surprised when I tell them that, with this gut cure, they could feel even better. Until they try it, of course. After all, you may think you feel good, but you don't realize what's possible until you start feeling even better.

## Healthy, energetic and slim

The fact is that we're all less healthy, less energetic and less slim than we could be if our gut was in optimum condition. Obesity is becoming our most common illness. The potential consequences of obesity are well known: an elevated risk of diabetes, cardiovascular disease and cancer. Worse, there is also a greater risk of complications from viral infections.

That's why I want to reach as many people as possible with this gut cure. In the next chapter, I'll explain how simple it is. It is definitely not just for people with severe symptoms. Especially those people who feel a little less energized, who are struggling with a few too many pounds, can experience considerable health benefits in the long run. They don't even have to make huge sacrifices to achieve it. That's the beauty of this cure, you don't have to exercise like crazy or deprive yourself of too many things. With a few small, simple interventions, you can continue to eat and drink whatever you want – all in moderation of course.

## Lighter living

A clean gut is the foundation of a healthy body. Because you don't eat any solid foods during the colon cleanse, it immediately results in weight loss. The anti-aging effect is especially noticeable in your skin, which looks fresher and younger afterwards. The long term result, however, is much more spectacular.

You can lose a few pounds with any diet, but, after a few months, you've probably gained them back plus a few extra as a bonus, the so-called yoyo effect. The result of a gut cleanse is quite different from that of a regular weight loss diet. The cravings that used to control your thoughts don't return. After a regular diet, you often tend to make up for what you feel you've missed out on. With the gut cleanse, this is not an issue. Frequent snack binges – those uncontrollable cravings for salt, sweet or fat – become a thing of the past. The cleaner your gut, the less your need for junk becomes. This reveals the intelligence of our "second brain", healthier food choices occur almost naturally. It also enhances your sense of taste and smell, making it less likely that you will seek out the extreme taste sensation that processed convenience foods offer.

You will not see the reduced inflammation in your body in the mirror, but you'll certainly feel it. The ailments you thought you had to learn to live with just disappear, along with the thought that these were just inherent to getting older, or to menopause, or to your stressful job – all things you had told yourself or had been led to believe.

The next chapter explains exactly what you can do to live lighter, with a healthier body and a clearer mind as a result. You'll be amazed how simple it is.

**Everyone overweight**

Obesity is a welfare phenomenon, but many nonsense claims are made about its cause. People are weak and cannot resist the temptation of food, it is often said. The only way to achieve a proper weight would be by following a health regime with plenty of exercise and appropriate nutrition. This is utter nonsense. What's the real issue? The thick biofilm in your intestines is damaging the intestinal wall, causing leaky gut syndrome. Food particles "leak" through tiny holes in the intestinal wall. The immune system is triggered when it detects these invaders and autoimmune responses occur, causing inflammation throughout the body and other tedious conditions. One of these conditions is insulin resistance, the preliminary stage of diabetes, which can lead to metabolic issues causing obesity.

The assumption that you should go on a diet and spend hours in the gym is a wrong one. With a cleansed gut, you can regain your health and continue to live the way you like, with moderate but tasty food that satisfies you sufficiently, regular treats and a glass of wine to go with it on occasion.

5

# The Gut Protocol: Getting Started

*The previous chapters dealt with the importance of a healthy gut and how to remove the biofilm, this one deals with the practical side. The gut protocol has countless health benefits the results speak for themselves. This chapter will also show you how simple it is. I'll take you through the process step by step – the rest is up to you. Ready to get started?*

There are many types of colon cleansing cures available. However, virtually nothing exists that actually removes the biofilm from both the large and small intestine. Even the very few options that are available have considerable disadvantages. With some there's the risk that the biofilm breaks open, releasing all the harmful bacteria at once – with damaging consequences. Others have a severe abrasive effect on the intestinal wall, which is already badly damaged by the presence of the biofilm. The cure described in the previous section has no adverse effect on the intestinal system. On the contrary, it's a very gentle method.

Another benefit is highlighted in this chapter:, it's a short cure which is very easy to complete. You don't have to follow tedious diets or feel hungry. All you have to do is replace your food with meal shakes for six days, the ingredients will do the rest. The shakes replace all other food, but provide ample nutrition. This will bring your digestion to a halt and allow the ingredients to kick in.

**Gut protocol versus fasting**

Intermittent fasting. Anyone interested in health has probably come across it at some point.

It's quite popular to restrict your food intake for a limited number of days. Some people, for example, eat normally for five days a week and only liquids for two days. Another option is eating all meals of the day within an 8-hour time frame. This is great if you want to lose a few pounds and it's excellent for your overall health. But the cause of health issues, the biofilm, is not addressed.

If you're familiar with fasting, some of the effects of the gut protocol will not be new to you. If you are new to this, it might be nice to know what to expect. First of all, the term "fasting" doesn't really apply to the cure. You are not eating any solid foods, but the similarities end there. Besides the cure itself, which is quite filling, you may eat cleansing soups based on vegetable broth, and you may drink vegetable and fruit juices as desired. In other words, you won't feel faint, dizzy or hungry for a moment. The well known energy dip associated with fasting, which occurs when blood sugar levels drop after a period without eating, is also absent. The great thing about the cure is that you will instantly start feeling more energetic during the cure days, and in most cases you won't have to adjust your lifestyle or work schedule.

## A regular rhythm

The great thing about the cure is that you can maintain a regular daily rhythm. The cure comes in boxes, one box for each day, containing seven sachets of powder that can be mixed with water or juice to make a shake. The seven daily shakes (three meals and four snacks) can be taken according to a fixed daily schedule and will leave you feeling quite full. You start your day with an early snack, breakfast an hour or so later, then a mid-morning snack, lunch, a mid-afternoon snack, dinner and a late snack. All in the form of a shake, but with the addition of spices and juices. You can vary endlessly. The result is that you don't feel like you're missing out on anything.

## The right moment

Considering doing the cure? There's no reason to wait until "the right time". The beauty of this gentle and targeted cleanse is that anyone can do it and while continuing to do whatever they normally do. It doesn't matter if you're doing it becase you have a particular complaint or simply because you want to be as healthy as possible, you'll be doing your body a favor. Remember, vague symptoms can be an indication of more serious issues, so it's never a bad time to do the cure.

Age is not a factor either. With age, inflammatory responses all over the body increase further and your defenses decrease, making you more susceptible to disease. This means there's a lot to gain, even later in life.

When your gut is in top condition, your ability to recover is better. You'll get rid of inflammations, bacterial infections or (contagious) diseases much faster if your immune system is working properly and isn't burdened by the effects of biofilm. Medical treatments also work better when you're otherwise in good shape.

In short, the cure is suitable for practically everyone. If you're experiencing some complaint or other, you'll see the biggest improvements. As long they follow the instructions are carefully, the colon cleanse can even be done by people with chronic illnesses for whom the usual ways of fasting are too strenuous or even dangerous.

Many people who do the cure have been struggling with misunderstood symptoms for years. Complaints the GP or specialists couldn't fix. These people had often tried all kinds of things including special diets, fasting cures, colon irrigation, medication and alternative therapies, often with limited success.

**Kickstart or maintenance**

The basic cure lasts six days, but there are also 3 day and 12 day cures available. The six day cure is suitable for anyone of normal weight or anyone who's slightly overweight. It rids your intestines of biofilm, restores intestinal flora and does wonders for your metabolism and organs. If you've never done a cure before, it's best to start with this one.

Over time, the biofilm will start to build up again along the intestinal wall. A maintenance cure is needed to maintain the health gains achieved. A three-day cure once every six to twelve months, or as needed, can serve this purpose. If you really don't see a chance to schedule a six-day cure for whatever reason, the three-day cure can provide some comfort. Indeed, a short cure is always better than no cure at all.

There's also a 12-day cure, for people who have many symptoms and really want or need to lose weight. It will give you an instant kickstart on weight loss. After that, your cleansed gut will help you achieve a healthy weight.

## Preparation

It's wise to prepare yourself, physically and mentally, in the days leading up to the cure. This marks the start of a new way of life and it's good to take a moment to grasp that. It's not something to dread, it's something to look forward to. My clients often refer to their life before and their life after the cure. So, it's safe to assume that something is going to change in your life – for the better.

Proper preparation will get you in the right mindset. After all, we're creatures of habit. Many behaviors are unconscious, and we thrive on regularity, predictability and routine. Anything familiar (even if not necessarily fun) is safe. On the other hand, any change can therefore subconsciously feel like a threat, even if it's a change for the better. Once you're aware of this you can understand where any reluctance is coming from and you can push past it more easily. Let it dawn on you that you're about to do something that's going to help you, and look forward to it. You're going to feel better and have fewer complaints.

It's best to schedule the first two cure days on a weekend. You'll need some time to adjust, so it makes sense to start at a more relaxed time. Should you feel a bit sluggish during the first day, which is perfectly normal, then you can rest in the comfort of your own home. In most cases, you'll feel much better on the second day and by the third day, Monday, you'll be fit to go to work.

## Cutting down on food

Start preparing your body two days before the cure. This will help smooth the transition to the first cure day. It also helps you to work towards the cure very consciously by taking extra good care of yourself right now.

Eat a little less on the first day of preparation, perhaps half of what you would normally eat. If you plan to lose a lot of weight, this is particularly recommended. Don't eat too many fatty foods or anything with too many carbohydrates either.

On the second day of preparation, eat food that's easily digestible. For example, fruit for breakfast, yogurt for lunch and soup for dinner. I also recommend that you phase out black tea and coffee during these days. After these preparations, you'll be all set for the start of a healthier and more energetic life.

## How does it work?

There is a box for each day. Each box contains three "meal" shakes, two wake-up-and-good-night shakes and two snack shakes.

The intake schedule is as follows, feel free to adjust the times according to your own schedule:

- Getting up (8 a.m.) – the first wake-up and good night shake.
- An hour later (9 a.m.) – the first meal shake.
- Mid-morning (10:30 a.m.) – the first snack.
- Lunchtime (12:30 p.m.) – the second meal shake.
- Mid-afternoon (3 p.m.) – the second snack.
- Dinner time (6 p.m.) – the third meal shake.
- Late in the evening (9 p.m.) – the second wake up and good night shake.

Start the day with a wake-up-and-good-night shake. This is a green colored shake packed with vitamins and minerals which ensures that you don't develop any deficiencies during the cure. After about an hour, take the first meal shake. The meal sachets contain the effective ingredients of the cure. You can skip the other sachets if it's too much for you, but the meal sachets are essential to success. They contain the okra powder and the fermented fiber of the palm tree bark.

You can prepare the shakes with water or non-pulp-containing juice. Use apple juice, for example, or any other kind of fruit juice or juice concentrate, preferably organic. Juice concentrate is a natural lemonade made from thickened fruit juice. It will last longer than a bottle of pure juice. You may also flavor the shakes with things like cinnamon, cocoa powder, stevia or honey.

After the first meal shake, your breakfast, take your first "snack" mid morning. This shake is designed to ensure you ingest the right fatty acids. Again, feel free to add something to suit your taste.

At midday, take the second meal shake, your lunch, and another snack shake mid afternoon. If you fancy something savory in the afternoon, you can dissolve a teaspoon of organic tomato puree in boiling water – add plenty of seasoning salt and pepper. You may develop a need for salt during the cure and it's fine to take that any time. A simple cup of warm water with some sea salt or Herbamare salt, such as a broth, is fine.

Take the last meal shake around dinnertime, again with an additive to taste. This doesn't have to be a fruity flavor every time, you can also prepare the shake with vegetable juice, just be sure there is no fiber in that either. Before bed, take the last wake-up-and-good-night shake, and you're done for the day.

Most of my clients feel perfectly full from all the day's shakes, plus the additional 6 cups of water or herbal tea. For some, it's even a bit too much. If this also applies to you, leave out the snack shakes, and if necessary, the wake-up and good-night shakes as well.

If you're having difficulty with the thickness or the flavor of the shake, you can also cut them into two portions. Take half a sachet each time, and mix it with the 400 ml of liquid you would normally use for the whole sachet. The shake is thinner that way and easier to ingest. If you prefer you can also eat the shake from a bowl with a spoon as if it were soup.

Play around with it, give yourself time to figure out how you prefer to take the cure and how you can adjust it to your liking. Once you've figured that out, it's quite easy to persevere. Just remember, it's not a three-star meal, it is a health cure.

The okra in the gut cure attracts huge amounts of moisture. Therefore, in addition to the three meal shakes, you need at least 6 to 9 cups of fluid to ensure better flow. Water, especially spring water, and herbal teas are best for this purpose. Otherwise you can just let the process take its course and get on with your daily activities. The only thing I would advise against are endurance sports. Your body is working too hard on other things to prepare for any marathon!

## What can you expect?

Nearly everyone starts feeling better during the cure. Still, it's good to realize, that a lot is happening in your body.

Your gut is in the midst of a major cleanse. Harmful substances are being disposed of in a safe way, without those toxins entering your blood. They disappear, along with the fibers of the cure and the biofilm, via the natural way out, without ever entering your blood or burdening your organs.

During this process, your metabolism is running at full speed. That takes energy. Your complaints may temporarily come into focus and you may experience them more intensely. Usually, you feel the very things that bothered you most and you want to get rid of. People suffering from eczema sometimes develop more symptoms for a while. Someone with irritable bowel syndrome may experience some extra rumbling in the abdomen. If you frequently suffer from headaches, they may temporarily get worse. Do make sure you're drinking plenty of fluids, because insufficient fluids can also cause headaches.

Trust that your body is merely responding to the cure and that it's working very hard to help you get rid of those symptoms in the longer term. The body may be a bit more sensitive for a while and this will manifest itself through your weaknesses. But that effect wears off quickly, so hang in there.

During the cure, you may also experience what I call "hyper-awareness". You temporarily become more aware of what's going on in your body. This can cause stings and aches to occur that make you think: "see, this isn't helping me, I better stop." Just remember, there's no harm in it and it certainly won't last the entire time. Fortunately, this only affects a small group of users.

The cure itself has been carefully formulated. It doesn't contain any gluten, added sugars, soy or lactose, so the shakes are also suited for people with food allergies and intolerances. The flavor of the meal shakes is neutral, and the enclosed instructions provide all kinds of tips on how to customize the shakes to your taste.

Never done a cure before? It can be quite challenging at first. The moment you stop eating, your whole body starts working hard to catch up on all sorts of overdue maintenance. Give yourself some time to adjust. You can take a bit of time off work if you prefer, but it's not necessary. I have seen people with tough jobs – firefighters, car mechanics, road workers – go through the cure effortlessly. In any case, make sure you get plenty of rest after work. Take a long bath or maybe get comfortable on the couch with a good book.

## What happens inside your body?

Once your digestion comes to a standstill, your body wants to perform all sorts of repair and clean up work that it hasn't gotten around to for years. In many people, the digestive system is so overloaded that digesting food has become an arduous task. The intestines are nothing but hollow muscles that work all day to transport the food mash from top to bottom as it is digested. This takes quite a bit of energy and in some cases it's such hard work that almost all the energy from the food goes straight back to the intestines. This manifests as fatigue, because the body simply lacks the energy for other activities.

So, once you stop eating, energy becomes available, and the body starts to repair itself. This so-called self-healing happens naturally, but does cause the existing health situation to be magnified. If there are tissues somewhere in the body that need urgent repair, the body directs a lot of energy there to perform the work. This means that you may become aware of a situation that you weren't aware of until then. For example, someone with mild rheumatism who doesn't have any pain symptoms yet may notice their joints swelling slightly. This is your body's healing mechanism, but if you don't know what's going on it might scare you a bit.

I once had a client who experienced heart problems during the cure, something that couldn't have been caused by the ingredients of the cure, because they don't enter the blood. The ingredients go straight into the biofilm, which is transported towards the exit. I referred this man to his doctor, and it became evident that he had a defect in one of his heart valves, something that had been there for a long time. Without the cure, it may have never been discovered and it might have killed him. His body wanted to fix it during the cure, and he felt it. Fortunately, he went straight to the doctor and had surgery the next day, after which he made a full recovery. At a later stage, he was able to do an entire cure without any problems.

Fortunately, this is the only time something like this happened in my practice, but it does indicate that the body wants to show you something during the cure. As soon as you realize this is a positive thing, you can relax and help the body resolve it. During the cure you may always apply other methods that are good for the body, different types of massage, reflex zone massage, acupuncture or homeopathic remedies and herbal teas for the liver and kidneys. A sauna session, however, is not a good idea as it may be too intense.

## Detoxification and other responses

Since you will not be consuming alcohol, coffee, black tea, or food with chemical additives during the cure, you may experience a variety of symptoms that indicate detoxification. Mild headaches are one of them. This is quite normal, and the best remedy is simply to drink more water or herbal teas specifically for the liver and kidneys. This benefits the detoxification process and makes it easier for your body to get rid of these toxins.

From time to time, there are people who experience severe headaches. This could suggest two possible causes. Firstly, if you are a heavy coffee drinker and you suddenly stop during the cure, your body will have to adjust. That adjustment can manifest itself as a fierce headache. It will go away after a few days, but sometimes it helps to have a single cup of coffee on that day.

A second possible cause has to do with the gallbladder. There are people who, without knowing it, have a gallbladder that's overfull. The gallbladder starts working really hard during the cure to empty itself, giving rise to what is known as bile colic which manifests itself as a severe headache together with nausea or even vomiting. This happens to a very small percentage of people, less than 0.5 percent. Should it happen to you, it's important to stop the cure and first do a liver cleanse according to the Andreas Moritz method. You can find more information about it online and there's also a description available on my website.

If you experience dizziness during the cure, this could be an indication that you had low blood sugar prior to the cure. This goes away on its own in the early days of the cure. For some people, however, it's a good idea to take three to six glasses of fruit juice a day during the cure to keep blood sugar levels stable.

## The cure and chronic conditions

The cure is completely safe for diabetics. It is important, however, to keep a close eye on blood sugar levels and if there are abnormal values, respond with insulin use. I have guided several diabetics through the cure, and they often needed much less insulin afterwards, some of them even none at all.

People who are taking medication should continue to do so as usual. If you need to take medication with a meal, it is important to do so with a wake-up-and-good-night shake and not with a meal shake. Anything ingested during meal shakes goes directly into the biofilm and is not absorbed into the blood. Therefore, don't take your medication just before, during or straight after a meal shake.

Be sure to check yourself regularly, for example if you're taking medication for high blood pressure. By doing the cure, your blood pressure usually naturally drops a little, so if you keep taking the normal dose of your medication, your blood pressure may become too low. Monitor your blood pressure and consult your doctor if it drops too far. The same applies to other medication, check yourself regularly (possibly in consultation with your doctor), especially if you're doing a six or twelve day cure.

## Tackling the biofilm

What happens in your body when you drink a meal shake is a miraculous process. Drink the shake immediately after preparing it or it will become too thick. The shake will then flow easily through your esophagus and stomach, smoothly entering the intestinal system and penetrating the biofilm. This causes the thin layer of biofilm to swell. This unique effect cannot be achieved in any other way. The biofilm is released and forms a kind of skin layer around the ingredients of the product you took during this cure. This comes out naturally with your bowel movements and looks like a sausage. The gut is left clean, and the fragile, dried-out intestinal wall can begin to repair itself.

What comes out is largely the product of the shakes. Surrounding it is the biofilm, which is transparent and microscopically thin but forms a firm membrane around the product. This process needs to be repeated for several days in a row before most of the biofilm disappears from the gut. Therefore, it is necessary to do the cure for at least three, but preferably six days. That way, you can be sure to get rid of as much biofilm as possible.

If you observe your stool, you'll witness the result of the cure. "Normal" poo can still be seen on the first day, but it changes in the following days. You know the excretion of the biofilm has started when you see a dark string from the intestinal cleansing product with a membrane around it which is the biofilm. Some observe this particular type of stool right on the first day. For others, it doesn't start until the second or third day.

The skin of biofilm looks like plastic wrap or a sausage skin. It can come out as one long string or strand, or a large number of short strands. Perhaps you'll need to go to the toilet a little more often and a little comes out each time, resembling regular diarrhea. Don't worry about it too much, everyone has a different rhythm. Your body is working hard. Even if many little pieces come out, the process is completely safe. The biofilm may come out in parts, but it will never disintegrate in the gut itself.

## What if nothing comes out?

Most people see a great deal of biofilm coming out during the cure, but there are also cases where nothing or almost nothing comes out. Sometimes clients call me to complain that they've gone through so much trouble with no effect. Of course, I understand their frustration. When you're putting in all that effort, you want to see results. If nothing comes out during the cure, it doesn't mean the cure didn't work. The cure will always work on anyone. When you take a meal shake, the contents always end up in the biofilm in your gut. As a result, it is moistened and detached from the intestinal wall. Measurements on hundreds of users in my practice have demonstrated this.

In some cases, people were already suffering from constipation before the cure. The released biofilm is not as thick as regular stool in the rectum, and for some people it needs a certain weight of filling for a bowel movement to occur. The biofilm itself lacks that weight and so the body won't release it immediately. This happens in about 20 percent of users. If the biofilm doesn't come out during the cure, it's no big deal. The cure still worked, but the biofilm won't come out until they start eating again. Then the biofilm gets mixed in with the stool and is no longer clearly visible.

If you'd rather get rid of the biofilm straight away during the cure, there is a solution. You can purchase magnesium sulfate (bitter salt) at the drugstore or pharmacy. If you dissolve one tablespoon of this in a glass of water and drink it, everything should come out. In fact, it induces a kind of artificial diarrhea. If, as is the case in some people, it still doesn't come out, a second glass of bitter salt is required two hours after the first. A word of warning, though, is to stay near a restroom.

This advice only applies to a small percentage of people, most will simply go through the cure without any real issues. Nevertheless, this is a period of peak performance for your body, and you need to give the body plenty of rest.

## A reset for your body

You'll feel different after the cure. Some people who start the cure become so excited they want to continue for a few more days. If you opted for the three-day cure, you may be motivated to continue until you've completed six days. By all means, go for it.

After the cure, especially if you've done a six or twelve day cure, it's important to slowly reestablish a normal eating pattern. If you need to lose weight, now is the time to start eating differently. Avoid rigorous dieting, it really won't do you any good. It's probably not necessary either. Simply eating differently is far more helpful.

Your cleansed gut can handle normal, healthy foods just fine, so you won't gain much weight again anytime soon. The rampant cravings you had were caused by a disturbed metabolism fueled by leaky gut syndrome. In conjunction with your brain, your gut was constantly sending signals to ingest more food. With that constant need for more food, which was never completely fulfilled, it was only natural to start looking for the extremes, foods that were even sweeter, even fattier, even saltier than you were already used to.

The cure induces a kind of reset. The irritated intestinal wall has calmed down and your metabolism has normalized. Your body is no longer screaming for vitamins to diminish inflammatory responses. Your taste buds have also undergone a "reset". You'll be amazed at how intense your sense of taste is now. So, hide the sugar and enjoy the pure flavors of real food.

## Start eating again

Be especially careful in those first few days after you finish not to overload your digestion. Prepare a delicious pan of soup in advance to enjoy on the first "build-up" day. Make sure it has been brewing for quite some time. The vegetables and possibly meat it contains should be thoroughly cooked.

Start the day with one or two soft boiled eggs or some yogurt. In the afternoon, have a bowl of that delicious soup. Smoothies and oatmeal are allowed too, of course. For dinner, some more soup and possibly a soft boiled potato. Wait a couple of days before eating fruit, which is a bit too intense for your gut in the beginning.

Eat roughly the same on the second day and add some more cooked vegetables. Raw vegetables are better saved for later, the intestines have to work too hard on them. Give your intestines some rest by avoiding alcohol and coffee as well.

In the days that follow, you can start off gently with fresh vegetables, fruits and small portions of protein sources, such as poached fish and grilled chicken. This is how you gradually build up your diet. You're probably no longer craving full plates and unhealthy snacks between meals, but you don't have to frantically count calories either. After all, obesity is not a matter of too many calories.

**The role of calories**

The biggest misconception about achieving a healthy weight is that you can achieve it by limiting your calorie intake per day. When your body receives fewer calories, it simply starts working a little less hard, in order to conserve energy. You'll end up losing weight of course, but you're disrupting your entire metabolism in the process. The body is a miracle of ingenuity, and your metabolism will eventually be restored. However, if you've done this for several years in a row – alternating crash diets with periods of normal or excessive eating – you're probably heavier than ever. You have developed a slow metabolism. That explains why you gain weight so quickly when you indulge just a little. Exercise becomes more difficult due to the excess weight, but also because your body resists attempts to drain it of even more energy. The only way to stay slim is a crash diet combined with strenuous exercise. However, there are some major objections to this.

First of all, it's not something you can sustain for a long time if you want to live an enjoyable life. Second, it's far from healthy. In fact, you're wearing yourself out, physically and mentally. Your organs suffer, your body goes into a kind of survival mode and will start "eating" itself by extracting substances from bones and muscles. In other words it is not a good idea. If you do nothing, though, you'll only gain more weight.

A disturbed metabolism can return to normal only through some kind of reset. Only then will you be able to stop counting calories worry free. Your second brain will automatically tell you when it has had enough. It produces hormones that signal a feeling of satiation. If your gut is littered with biofilm, it fails to do so. That's why, after the cure, you can finally achieve and maintain your ideal weight, simply by adjusting your lifestyle instead of following a strenuous diet.

## Life after the cure

By now, you must be wondering what results people are getting from this cure. There is only one way to find out and that is to follow the cure yourself. The health outcomes achieved vary from person to person, but certain results can be observed across the board. People experience more energy and fewer feelings of dejection. They feel better mentally. In fact, for some, their depression disappears altogether. Belly size usually decreases, and people experience a more supple body.

Some also sleep better and taste their food better. They have fewer cravings for unhealthy foods, sugar, alcohol and coffee after the cure, making it the perfect time to create new, healthier eating habits.

Some people already feel tremendously energized during the cure. They start cleaning and fixing up the house, clearing out the garage, etc. If you have the energy, go for it. Don't overdo it though, take a break every now and then and have a nice cup of herbal tea or tomato broth.

The above results are reported by many users, but individually they can vary greatly. Once you're eating again, it is wise to take it one step further and cleanse your body's cells by taking a remedy to replenish your intestinal flora. More on that in the next chapter.

## Who would be better off not doing the cleanse?

The gut cure is highly beneficial for most people. A few circumstances exist, however, where I would advise against doing the cure. Firstly, the cure is not recommended for pregnant women, small children and people who are severely debilitated.

People with severe intestinal diseases are also better off not doing the cure. These individuals actually need this cure the most, but for them, the risk of complications is too high. If you suffer from a gut condition that involves minor bleeding, such as Crohn's disease, the "crusts" from that bleeding can become trapped in the biofilm. When the biofilm becomes detached from the intestinal wall, it can start bleeding again.
If you're not sure if the cure is safe for you, it's wise to consult your doctor. Thankfully, there's only a very small group of people for whom we would not recommend the cure.

## User experiences

Two users of the gut cure share their experiences below. These testimonials will give you an impression of what to expect.

### *Years of fatigue*

*I struggled for years with mono, mycoplasma and Lyme disease and was recently diagnosed with candida as well. For a long time, I was burdened with tremendous fatigue and persistent low energy levels. I had tried everything from antibiotics to homeopathy, bioresonance, mesology and light therapy, until I read the following phrase somewhere: "death lurks in the gut."*

*So I tried the three day cure. The first day I had a headache and felt hungry. I didn't like the shakes' penetrating flavor and smell of peas. I solved that by splitting it into two servings and mixing in some organic juice.*

*The first day I had no stool, so I feared that I'd wasted my money. Thankfully, a large chunk of the biofilm came out on the second morning. I was so happy. It worked after all! I finally got rid of that dirty mess in my body that has probably been keeping me tired for years. Later in the day, some smaller pieces came out.*

*I had some mild cramps at night, and by the third day, my bowels were rumbling away, with cramps and several smaller stools. All in all, the cure was quite manageable. Over the next few weeks, I'm going to let my gut flora recover properly with additional remedies. I'll definitely repeat the cure in the future and I'm hopeful that this is the first significant step towards my full recovery.*

***Relieved within 5 hours***

*I had already followed several cleansing cures before, but never have I had such a dirty mass come out of my bowels! To be honest, I was a little hesitant when I first read about this method of colon cleansing on the website. That's why I only followed a three-day course the first time. After all, I didn't know how my body was going to react, because I have very weak adrenal glands (close to Addison's disease) and a slow thyroid. The shake sachets are also quite costly, so I wanted to be sure that it worked. Stories are circulating on the internet that it's not biofilm coming out during the cure but merely the gel mass from the sachets. And that this product mainly empties your wallet instead of your gut. That's why I was a bit hesitant. Still, the experiences of other users convinced me, and I decided to give it a try.*

*Yesterday was my last day of the three day cure. I went to the bathroom fifteen times, the biofilm was rushing out of me. On the first day, a 3 ft long biofilm came out after only five hours. I had taken the first sachet at nine o'clock and by two o'clock it was already happening.*

*I had a little trouble with my sugar levels the first day, but I solved this the next few days by replacing half the water with organic fruit juice each time. And I ate a boiled apple twice a day. Drinking those nine extra cups of water each day was also a challenge.*

*I stayed home from work because I felt too feeble. Next time, I'll do it when I have some time off. I was shocked, though, that there was so much junk in my intestines. I only eat healthy organic foods with very few sugars. I now have much less eczema and itchy skin. As it turns out, your health is clearly determined in the gut, for the most part anyway. All in all, it was a positive experience that I will definitely repeat in the future.*

## Summary

Doing this cure is like embarking on a new adventure. One where you can learn a great deal about the way your body works. The cure itself is quite manageable with the meal replacements and has the advantage that you don't have to cook. You can even spice up the contents of the sachets to make them more appealing. If detoxification symptoms occur, follow the tips in this book to reduce them. It is important that you cut down on your meals in the days before the cure, and carefully build them up again afterwards. The period immediately after the cure is a good time to adjust your diet and start eating more healthily to maintain a better weight.

# 6

# A Clean Gut, Now What?

*A lot has happened in your body after such a huge clean up! Once you've completed the cure, you'll find it was well worth it. Most people feel better after only a few days as they become more energized and, above all, more clear-headed. Some sleep much better, feel less depressed and have a renewed zest for life. For some, certain physical complaints or discomforts disappear. Naturally, you want these effects to last for as long as possible. With just a few minor lifestyle adjustments, you can accomplish great health gains. This chapter will reveal how. Your body will be grateful.*

## The result in your gut

After the cure, the biofilm in your gut is largely gone. This is truly a milestone for your body, because it has never before had the opportunity to get rid of that biofilm. Despite this wonderful result, it is also good to realize that without further maintenance, it will not necessarily last.

As you read at the beginning of the book, biofilm can be compared to plaque on your teeth. And just like with your teeth, you need to remove that layer regularly, so it doesn't cause any damage. Plaque on your teeth grows much faster than biofilm in your gut, but sooner

or later that biofilm too will start to grow again. How soon it returns depends on what you do now to prevent new growth.
Keeping your gut in top condition is vital to your overall health and fortunately not that difficult. Put some effort into it and you'll be rewarded with more energy, clarity and pleasant tranquility without relapsing to the pre-cure situation.

There are people who feel that they've already done enough for their health by doing the cure. Of course, every step you take is already pure gain. Below, I'll provide a variety of tips for healthy living after the cure. What you choose to fit into your life is up to you.

## Pay attention to nutrition

The post-cure period is the ideal time to revisit your old eating habits. How much sugar, gluten, dairy and food additives did you ingest each day? Were you eating enough fresh vegetables, fruits and homemade meals?

It's quite understandable if you've slipped up a bit in this area. There are so many ready made products, snacks and fast foods available nowadays. These are precisely the products, however, that your gut is not so fond of. So what are healthy choices? Are you struggling to make this distinction? A handy rule of thumb is to imagine your great-grandmother walking through the supermarket today: which products would she recognize and which not? Anything that she would fail to identify is basically something you'd better not eat. To put that another way, anything still resembling the form in which it occurs in nature is the healthiest for you.

Your gut is programmed to digest fresh vegetables, fruits, meat or fish, from which you can prepare your own delicious meals. Anything overly processed, such as fried foods and foods with many artificial additives is not very good for your gut.

This is not to say that you should go on a rigorous diet immediately, that would usually be far too complicated and difficult to maintain. Putting a little more thought into what you eat – more fresh produce, fewer snacks, no more McDonald's for example – is already a win. A practical guideline to live by is the 80-20 rule. Eat a healthy, balanced diet for 80 percent of the time and allow yourself to enjoy some of your favorite foods, in moderation, for the remaining 20 percent. That way, you can indulge yourself once in a while and you don't have to worry about not being able to eat anything tasty at all anymore.
Which, by the way, is not to say that healthy food isn't delicious. Check out health food stores, which actually sell tasty products that are not bad for you. It's quite possible to make lifestyle changes without missing out on too much. If you keep things enjoyable, it's more likely you'll stick to it.

## Repair the gut wall

After you've completed the gut cure, it's advisable to help your gut repair itself. Although the intestinal wall will be much cleaner than before, it will still be slightly inflamed due to the long-standing presence of the biofilm. You can completely restore this after the gut cure by using a remedy that has the something called humic acid as its main ingredient.

Humic acid is formed by bacteria in the soil and can be very healing when ingested. Its structure is too large to pass through the intestinal wall. Therefore, it remains in the gut and has a healing effect on the intestinal wall. You can take it for one to two months, while doing your best not to irritate the intestinal wall too much by eating unhealthy foods, otherwise it's a futile exercise. A gut can only become irritated by what you eat. Therefore, new eating habits combined with the humic acid works very well if you want to get your intestinal wall in optimum condition.

## Improve the bacterial balance

Once your intestinal walls have recovered somewhat, this is the ideal time to improve your gut flora. Ideally, we have over four pounds (yes, really!) of good bacteria in our intestines. It's important to keep this up to standard. If there are too few good bacteria, or too many bad bacteria in the gut, all sorts of health problems can arise such as a malfunctioning immune system, low vitamin production, allergies, rheumatism and even obesity.

Quite a few products exist to supplement benign gut bacteria, under the label *probiotics*, "pro" meaning "for", and "bios" meaning "life". Various types of probiotics exist, and these have different functions in your body. The human body has over a thousand different species of good gut bacteria, so if you take any probiotic product, the newcomers will usually encounter peers and fit right in. There are also probiotic products available which are specifically designed to further strengthen and support your intestinal wall. There is even a *gut repair kit* on the market for this purpose. Want to know which products I think are most suitable? On my website marionschaatsbergen.com you'll find more information.

## Drink plenty

To keep the gut properly hydrated, it's important to drink enough water every day. Coffee, tea, soft drinks and alcoholic beverages do not count towards that, quite the contrary. However, and most people don't know this, herbal tea *does* count as water for the body. Tea made from a single type of herb, such as chamomile, nettle, mint and so on, has the same effect on the body as pure water.

Some people have the habit of drinking one large glass full of water three times a day, in order to ingest at least a quarter gallon of fluids. Drinking large amounts of water at once is rather useless, it will simply be drained to the kidneys, which doesn't do your body much good. Your body can absorb a little over a cup of water into its cells per hour. So, drinking one cup of herbal tea per hour is actually an ideal way to keep your hydration levels up.

## Opt for pure water

Traces of many chemicals found in the atmosphere enter our drinking water. Although this is legally allowed up to a certain level, that doesn't mean the amounts below that level are completely harmless to you. Water treatment plants are also having an increasingly difficult time filtering out the large amounts of drugs, medication and other harmful things that people urinate into the sewer system. These residues end up in surface water after treatment, and eventually in our drinking water.
The way we transport our water also plays a role. Our drinking water travels from the waterworks to our homes through plastic or metal pipes. Many old houses even have old lead piping, allowing small particles of this toxic metal to get into the water. Plastic and copper pipes also release particles into the water that eventually comes out of your tap.

In short, our water is not as pure as many people think. For this reason, an important question is how you can get your hands on the purest water possible. There are many water purifiers on the market. Take, for example, the common filter jugs. A nice and accessible idea, but unfortunately water that is not forced through a filter under pressure is not properly filtered. These common filter jugs don't make a real difference in terms of water quality, because the water just runs through.

A good carbon filter on your faucet is already a step in the right direction. There are also water filters that you can connect directly to the water supply system. If these filters are changed regularly, they provide well-filtered water.

## Distilled water

In addition to filtration, there is another water treatment method available, distillation. A water distiller converts water into vapor. During the evaporation process, the contaminants in the water are left behind in the boiling chamber in solid form. The distiller then cools the evaporated water, returning it to its liquid state and providing you with the purest water there is. Water distillation mimics the way the Earth naturally purifies and redistributes water. It evaporates from the Earth's surface and forms clouds, before returning the water to the earth through rain, snow, and hail. This is a purification system as nature intended.

There are many types of distillers on the market, in various price ranges. The price gap can mainly be attributed to the ease of use, not the resultant water quality, making distilled water easily accessible. Once the water is distilled, it no longer contains any minerals. So, when you opt for distilled water, you can add a liquid multimineral supplement to keep your mineral levels up. Pour the distilled water in a glass or stainless steel bottle for on-the-go.
Popular plastic bottles are actually not that great for drinking water. Plastic usually contains plasticizers, a highly toxic chemical compound that leaks into the water. Be sure to use a bottle where that doesn't happen.

## Supplements

Once you've started working to restore the gut wall and bacterial balance after the cure, your gut will work significantly better than before. You'll definitely notice it in your overall energy level, your appearance and skin, your fitness, your resistance and simply in the way you feel. Health may start with a healthy gut, but your body needs more. A healthy gut wall doesn't instantly improve the condition of the rest of those billions of body cells. In particular, people who have been dealing with health issues related to bodily pollution for years need an extra push to address that as well. Highly effective supplements are available for this purpose. I'll list the most important ones below.

## Purify your body cells as well

Years of pollution are typically not limited to your gut. Throughout your body, toxins have accumulated in all kinds of tissues and organs as well. How can you effectively cleanse the rest of your body and get it in better shape? A naturally produced substance called fulvic acid is available for this purpose. It's the only substance I know that drains all the aforementioned chemical residues, even mercury, from the body.

Fulvic acid is extracted from ancient earth layers and is the result of a long process of decomposition by fungi and bacteria. It has the special characteristic of being able to transport pollution out of the cells and release nutrition into them. It's actually a missing link in our diet, nature intended for us to ingest it frequently with our plant-based diet. Due to modern farming methods, however, tis lacking from the vegetables we eat.

Fortunately, it's being extracted from the soil and marketed. It is important, however, that you purchase the purest quality available. Some varieties are contaminated. More information about the "clean" variety can be found on my website.

Of all the tips I give here for a healthy life after the cure, this one – combined with a healthy diet – is the most important. It is also very easy to implement, all you have to do is put a few drops of fulvic acid in a few glasses of the water you drink every day and the effect will be enormous.

## Vitamin and mineral requirements

In order to function properly, your body needs a certain number of vitamins and minerals on a daily basis. A huge misconception exists that if you eat healthily you will automatically get enough of them. That may have been true at one time in the very distant past, but those days are long gone. A world free of all the aforementioned pollution, that's what our bodies are made for. The food of our earliest ancestors is the food that nature intended for us: leafy greens, roots and turnips, fruits, insects and, very occasionally, a rabbit or a fish when they could get their hands on one. Pretty much the same diet monkeys have to this day. This diet contained all the vitamins and minerals people need. The liver and kidneys of our distant ancestors were not burdened much, because no chemicals needed to be removed from the body besides the body's own natural wastes.

Even though our bodies are not built for it, we are ingesting toxins in large quantities today. At the same time, our food has become increasingly depleted of nutrients due to modern production methods. For this reason, the body needs additional vitamins to neutralize and remove the toxins from the body.

Considerable deficiencies can build up due to both the toxic load on the body, which has to work extremely hard to counteract this, and our deficient diet. In short, our need for supplemental vitamins and minerals is huge.

## The right supplements

Supporting your body with additional vitamins and minerals is essential. There is a complicating factor here: many supplements on the market are not absorbed very well by the body. Your body is used to extracting vitamins and minerals from your food and converting them into a certain form that allows the body to properly absorb them into the blood and then into the cells. Unfortunately, with factory-made vitamins and minerals, only a small portion of the active ingredient is absorbed into the blood, so most of it actually never reaches the body's cells.

## Liposomal

Fortunately, we are a resourceful species and have found a way around this, too. There are supplements available that can be absorbed directly into the body's cells because they are "wrapped" in a type of fat globule. This fat globule, called a liposome, has exactly the same structure as our cell walls. These liposomal supplements ("lipo" means "fat") are recognized by the body as being internally produced. The body does produce its own kind of liposomes in the digestive system and anything that looks like this is absorbed well.

The fat globule is not torn apart in the digestive tract and doesn't need to be processed by the body. It enters the blood – still completely intact – and is transported to the body's cells, where the globule fuses with the cell wall. In that process, it releases its contents into the cell. This is a brilliant system with a double advantage: not only are the vitamins and minerals released into the cell immediately, but the cell wall also renews and rejuvenates itself with the substance of which the fat globule is made.

These liposomal supplements come in liquid and in capsule form, the capsules being of better quality and slightly easier to use. Included in this type of liposomal supplements is a multivitamin-mineral supplement, making it very easy to support your body with just one capsule per day.

So you see, it's definitely possible to give your body exactly what it needs to regain optimum health. All you need to know is how. Visit my website for more information on these products.

## Summary

After the cure, the time has come to take the next step and focus on the well-being of your gut. Improved nutrition, pure water, gut remedies and supplements can help you with this. Implementing all of this at once might be a bit much, so you can also decide to just build up slowly. Take one step at a time and make small changes gradually. Among all the advice given, there is bound to be something for everyone, something that's not too complicated and suits your lifestyle. Work on this first, and once you experience the positive effects it has on your body, you'll be motivated to keep going – to achieve true health, from within.

# Epilogue

This book reveals how our gut works, what it needs to function properly and how it becomes polluted. Our bodies are designed to live a natural life and process natural foods. In today's society, however, our bodies come into contact with a huge number of artificial substances on a daily basis. These chemicals cause acidification in the body, leading to overgrowth of harmful bacteria which form the biofilm in the gut. Hence, the circle of illness is complete.

In the 35 plus years I have been in practice guiding people to better health, it has become clear to me that it was mostly the lack of knowledge about the ins and outs of the body that caused people to neglect their own bodies. Time and again I received the same response from my clients when I gave them the right information, "why has no one ever explained this to me before?"

With this book, I want to demonstrate that you can take responsibility for your own health. Knowledge is power. The more you know about your own body and your health, the more you can take control. With this information you have a choice.

Unfortunately, hardly anyone knows anything about the biofilm in the gut, so there is still much work to be done to change this. My personal mission is to make sure that as many people as possible gain access to this information and, more importantly, take action.

This book is the first in a series that aims to help people work towards better health, fitness, optimum weight and anti-aging. This series could serve a work of reference on every aspect of the body and how to maintain it in a simple and natural way without going on the "tree-hugging" tour. Everything I describe can be incorporated into a normal lifestyle without crash dieting. Simply having the right knowledge of the right products can get you very far.

The unique product I have mentioned in this book, which allows you to remove the biofilm in your gut without damaging the intestinal wall, is readily available online. You can find more information about suppliers and where to buy the product on my website marionschaatsbergen.com which also contains articles on various health topics which interest me. By the way, I do not give personal advice on the site, but I do provide guidance on how to find a therapist who can help you in your personal journey.

# Bibliography


***Digestive function:***

Baillie-Hamilton, Paula. *The Detox Diet*. Penguin Michael Joseph, London 2002

Enders, Giulia. *Gut: the inside story of our body's most under-rated organ.* Scribe Publications, London 2016

Kiontke, Dr. Siegfried, Mechthild Rex-Najuch, Dr. Hartmut Horn, *Betriebstemperatur 37° Celsius*, VITATEC Verlagsgesellschaft mbH 2015 See: https://www.betriebstemperatur-37-grad.de

Wright, Jonathan V. and Lane Lenard, *Why stomach acid is good for you,* Rowman & Littlefield 2001

Website of the Dutch Stomach Liver Bowel Foundation: https://www.mlds.nl/gezonde-buik/hoe-werkt-de-spijsvertering/

Website of the Medisch Diagnostisch Centrum IJsselland: http://www.mdlcentrum.nl/page.php?ID=55

Information platform about health: https://www.gezondheidsplein.nl/menselijk-lichaam/darmen/item45059

Website of the National Institute of Diabetes and Digestive and Kidney Diseases, see: www.niddk.nih.gov/health-information/health-statistics/digestive-diseases

Website of the Centers for Disease Control and Prevention, see: https://www.cdc.gov/chronicdisease/index.htm

***The gut as the second brain:***

Kessel, Anne Van. *Manipulerende microben.* Kennislink, January 12, 2016 See: https://www.nemokennislink.nl/publicaties/manipulerende-microben/

Voormolen, Sander. *Bacteriën communiceren met zenuwstelsel in de darm.* NRC, February 12, 2020

***Planet pollution:***

Legler, Juliette and Hanna Disza. *Tracing Endocrine Disrupting Compounds in Human Amniotic Fluid*. Environmental Science & Technology, December 17, 2019, Volume 53, Number 24

*Scientists categorize Earth as a 'toxic planet'*. SciNews, February 7, 2017 See: https://phys.org/news/2017-02-scientists-categorize-earth-toxic-planet.html

***Air pollution and electromagnetic radiation:***

International scientists on electromagnetic radiation: https://emfscientist.org/

***Water pollution:***

Allaire, Maura. Wu, Haowei. Lall, Upmanu. National trends in drinking water quality violations, Volume 115, Number 9, February 12, 2018. See: https://www.pnas.org/doi/10.1073/pnas.1719805115

Cohen, Li. EPA finds more than 9 million lead pipes supplying drinking water throughout the US. CBS News. April 5, 2022. See: https://www.cbsnews.com/news/epa-more-than-9-million-lead-pipes-drinking-water-us/

***Obesity and eating habits:***

Lee, Hong Kyu. Pak, Youngmi. *Persistent Organic Pollutants, Mitochondrial Dysfunction, and Metabolic Syndrome*. Wiley 2018. (pp. 691-707) See: https://onlinelibrary.wiley.com/doi/10.1002/9781119329725.ch44

Figure 2.1: https://www.researchgate.net/figure/US-synthetic-chemical-production-and-prevalence-of-diabetes-of-total-population-and_fig1_323379141

Kelishadi, Roya, Parinaz Poursafa and Fahimeh Jamshidi. *Role of Environmental Chemicals in Obesity: A Systematic Review on the Current Evidence*. Journ Environ Public Health. 2013; 896789 See: ncbi.nlm.nih.gov/pmc/articles/PMC3687513.

***Nutritional value of fruits and vegetables:***

Newark, Esther G. Dirt Poor. *Have Fruits and Vegetables Become Less Nutritious?* Scientific American, April 27, 2011

Hogervorst, Linda. *Bevat onze voeding minder voedingsstoffen dan vroeger?* Gezondheidsnet.nl, April 12, 2018:

https://www.gezondheidsnet.nl/groente-en-fruit/bevat-onze-voeding-minder-voedingsstoffen-dan-vroeger

Deliso, Meredith. Only 1 in 10 adults eating enough fruits and vegetables, CDC finds. ABC News. January 7, 2022. See: https://abcnews.go.com/Health/10-adults-eating-fruits-vegetables-cdc-finds/story?id=82117939

***Infertility and contaminated amniotic fluid:***

Dusza, Hanna M., Elwin Janssen, Rakesh Kanda and Juliette Legler. *Method Development for Effect-Directed Analysis of Endocrine Disrupting Compounds in Human Amniotic Fluid*. Environ. Sci. Technol. 2019, 53, 24, 14649-14659. October 4, 2019

Kasteren, Joost van. *De kwaliteit van het mannelijk zaad*. Kennislink, 30 July 1996
See: https://www.nemokennislink.nl/publicaties/de-kwaliteit-van-het-mannelijk-zaad/

***Inflamed intestines and biofilm:***

Agarwal, Vishnu et al. *Prevention of Candida albicans biofilm by plant oils*. Mycopathologia. 165 (1): 13 – 19

Macfarlane, S. and J.F. Dillon. *Microbial biofilms in the human gastrointestinal tract*. Journal of Applied Microbiology. May 2007, 102 (5): 1187 – 1196

Macfarlane, Sandra et al. *Colonization of Mucin by Human Intestinal Bacteria and Establishment of Biofilm Communities in a Two-Stage Continuous Culture System*. Appl Environ Microbiol. November 2005; 71(11): 7483 – 7492

Rogers, A.H. *Molecular Oral Microbiology*. Caister Academic Press 2008. 65 – 108

Turnbaugh, Peter J. et al. *An obesity-associated gut microbiome with increased capacity for energy harvest*. Nature. December 2006; 444: 1027 – 1031

Independent knowledge about intestinal health from the Nutrikennis Foundation:
https://www.nutrikennis.nl/biofilm/

***Various illnesses:***

*Shaw, J. Raw and Red-Hot: Could inflammation be the cause of myriad chronic conditions?* Harvard Magazine 2019 May- June

**Alzheimer's disease:**

Website World Health Organization: https://www.who.int/news-room/fact-sheets/detail/dementia, March 15, 2023

Ellison, James M. *Gut Bacteria and Brains: How the Microbiome Affects Alzheimer's Disease*. BrightFocus.org. August 24, 2021

See: https://www.brightfocus.org/alzheimers/article/gut-bacteria-and-brains-how-microbiome-affects-alzheimers-disease

Kowalski, Karol and Agata Mulak. *Brain-Gut-Microbiota Axis in Alzheimer's Disease*. Journal of neurogastroenterology and motility. January 2019. 25(1): 48 – 60
See: https://www.ncbi.nlm.nih.gov/pmc/articles/PMC6326209/

**Arthrosis:**

Saunders, David and Steven Burdette. *Infections Associated with Anti Tumor Necrosis Factor (TNF) Medications*. Antimocrobe.org. Undated
See: http://www.antimicrobe.org/e58.asp

**Asthma and COPD**

Website of the Dutch Lung Foundation: https://www.longfonds.nl/astma/alles-over-astma/symptomen-astma

*Ik heb COPD. Wat kan ik doen?* Workbook developed by Pharos and the Dutch Lung Fund, in collaboration with NHG and V&VN. Available for free download: https://www.pharos.nl/factsheets/copd-en-beperkte-gezondheidsvaardigheden/NHIS Adult Summary Health Statistics, website CDC: https://data.cdc.gov/d/25m4-6qqq, March 27, 2023

**Autoimmune diseases:**

Radboud University Medical Center: https://www.radboudumc.nl/patientenzorg/aandoeningen/auto-immuunziektes/wat-zijn-auto-immuunziektes

**Anemia:**

C. Gasche, C., M.C.E. Lomer, I. Cavill and G. Weiss. *Iron, anaemia, and inflammatory bowel diseases*. In: Gut. 2004 Aug; 53(8), pp. 1190–1197. See: https://www.ncbi.nlm.nih.gov/pmc/articles/PMC1774131/

**Intestinal diseases:**

Dutch Stomach Liver Bowel Foundation: https://www.mlds.nl/onze-darmen-in-feiten-en-cijfers/

Irritable Bowel Syndrome Advocacy Group: https://www.pdsb.nl/nieuws/onze-darmen-in-feiten-en-cijfers

**Depression:**

Ohlsson,L . A. Gustafsson, E. Lavant, K. Suneson, L. Brundin, Å. Westrin,

L. Ljunggren, and D. Lindqvist. *Leaky gut biomarkers in depression and suicidal behaviour*. Acta psychiatrica Scandinavica. February 2019. 139(2), pp. 185–193
See: https://www.ncbi.nlm.nih.gov/pmc/articles/PMC6587489/

Depression statistics, website CDC: https://www.cdc.gov/nchs/fastats/depression.htm

**Diabetes:**

De Kort, S., D. Keszthelyi and A.A.M. Masclee. *Leaky Gut and Diabetes Mellitus: What Is the Link?* Obesity reviews: an official journal of the International Association for the Study of Obesity. June 2011. 12(6), pp. 449 – 58
See: https://pubmed.ncbi.nlm.nih.gov/21382153/

Dansinger, Michael. *How Does Caffeine Affect Your Blood Sugar?* WebMD Medical Reference, 4 May 2019. See: https://www.webmd.com/diabetes/diabetes-and-caffeine

Swithers, Susan E. *Artificial Sweeteners Produce the Counterintuitive Effect of Inducing Metabolic Derangements*. Trends in endocrinology and metabolism: TEM. September 2013. 24(9), pp. 431 – 41. See: https://pubmed.ncbi.nlm.nih.gov/23850261/

National Diabetes Statistics Report 2022, website CDC: https://www.cdc.gov/diabetes/health-equity/diabetes-by-the-numbers.html

**Cancer:**

International Agency for Research on Cancer (IARC) and the US National Toxicology Program (NTP): https://www.cancer.org/cancer/cancer-causes/general-info/known-and-probable-human-carcinogens.html

Saggioro, Alfredo. *Leaky Gut, Microbiota, and Cancer: An Incoming Hypothesis*. Journal of clinical gastroenterology. Nov-Dec 2014.48 Suppl 1:S62-6.
See: https://pubmed.ncbi.nlm.nih.gov/25291131/

Cancer Data and Statistics, website CDC: https://www.cdc.gov/cancer/dcpc/data/index.htm

**Multiple sclerosis:**

Kirby, Trevor O. and Javier Ochoa-Repáraz. *The Gut Microbiome in Multiple Sclerosis: A Potential Therapeutic Avenue*. Medical Sciences (Basel, Switzerland). September 2018. 6(3): 69.
See: https://www.ncbi.nlm.nih.gov/pmc/articles/PMC6163724/

Koskie, Brandi. Multiple Sclerosis: Facts, Statistics and You. Healthline, September 7, 2022. See: https://www.healthline.com/health/multiple-sclerosis/facts-statistics-infographic

**Parkinson's disease:**

Dutch Brain Foundation: https://www.hersenstichting.nl/hersenaandoeningen/parkinson/

Caudle, W. Michael, Thomas S. Guillot, Carlos R. Lazo, and Gary W. Miller. *Industrial toxicants and Parkinson's disease*. Neurotoxicology. March 2012. 33(2), pp. 178 – 188.
See: https://www.ncbi.nlm.nih.gov/pmc/articles/PMC3299826/

LeBrun, Nancy. How common is psoriasis? May 4, 2022. See: https://www.verywellhealth.com/how-common-is-psoriasis-5220875

**Psoriasis:**

Haines Ely, P. *Is Psoriasis a Bowel Disease? Successful Treatment With Bile Acids and Bioflavonoids Suggests It Is*. Clinics in dermatology. May-June 2018.36(3), pp. 376 – 389.
See: https://pubmed.ncbi.nlm.nih.gov/29908580/

**Rheumatism:**

RA Statistics: https://rheumatoidarthritis.net/what-is-ra/ra-statistics

**Allergies and food intolerances:**

Kingsley, Patrick and Ian Stoakes. *The Nutron Diet*. Penguin Books London 1994

Roeline Bos. *Waarom is een pinda-allergie zo dodelijk vergeleken met andere allergieën?* Quest, January 28, 2020

Allergies, website CDC: https://www.cdc.gov/nchs/fastats/allergies.htm

Printed in Great Britain
by Amazon

41672163R00076